A WOMAN'S Guide to KEEPING PROMISES

Other Books by Judith Rolfs

52 Ways to Keep Your Promises:
As a Man, As a Husband, As a Father
(coauthored with Wayne Rolfs)

A Parent's Treasurebox of
Ideas for Preschoolers

Dealing with Cancer

Questions and Answers About
God's Healing Today

Love Always, Mom

Hey! I've Got Cancer

Hey! I've Got AD(H)D

A WOMAN'S *Guide* to KEEPING PROMISES

*Fifty-Two Ways to Choose
Happiness and Fulfillment*

Judith Rolfs

Grand Rapids, MI 49501

Published by Kregel Resources, an imprint of Kregel Publications, P.O. Box 2607, Grand Rapids, MI 49501. Kregel Resources provides timely and relevant resources for Christian life and service. Your comments and suggestions are valued.

Cover design: Alan G. Hartman
Book design: Nicholas G. Richardson

Library of Congress Cataloging-in-Publication Data
Rolfs, Judith
   A woman's guide to keeping promises: fifty-two ways to choose happiness and fulfillment / Judith Rolfs.
      p.   cm.
   1. Women—Prayer-books and devotions—English.
2. Christian life. 3. Devotional calendars. I. Title
BV4844.R65   1996   248.8'43—dc20   96-16867
                                                            CIP

ISBN 0-8254-3627-3

Printed in the United States of America
1 2 3 4 5 / 00 99 98 97 96

To
the countless women
who have helped me run toward the vision,
and to my daughters, Tamara and Pamela,
and daughter-in-law, Kathy,
the next baton carriers.

Contents

Introduction

"Write the vision and make it plain on the tablets,
that he may run who reads it."—Habakkuk 2:2

Women are so precious to God, yet our culture has many of us running at an unbelievable pace through the maze of daily life. Having often been a "runner" myself, I know how easy it is to become numb to the deeper realities of our spiritual and emotional life. When that numbness sets in, we miss sharing what's truly important with our husbands and children.

I went to graduate school to become an "expert" at counseling families and found my academic training didn't fully equip me for the job. Instead, I found that the principles of Scripture and the grace of God are what change lives. So I have written down some of the most useful principles I've learned over the last couple of decades of counseling women and families in order to "make the vision plain" for those who run.

The subjects for keeping promises found in many of these fifty-two ways could be the topics for an entire book. Most of us, however, don't have time to read fifty-two books, so I've extracted the essence and made it plain and practical. These truths apply to us whether we're new Christians or mature Christian women who've spent a lifetime with our Lord. They'll help us whether we work inside or outside the home.

We All Make Promises

What promises have you made? If you're a Christian woman, you implied a promise when you asked Christ to be Lord of your life—to love Him and serve Him. If you're a married woman, you made promises of love and faithfulness to your husband on your wedding day. If you're a parent, when you first held that tiny baby, you probably made an unspoken promise to love and protect this gift of life. Now you want to keep each of your promises. I pray that these "Ways" will help you.

As I wrote each one of these sections, I was nudged to shape up my own act—I'm still in process, too. But I do know that what's in here

9

works. These ways have been tested and held true. My counseling clients who have applied these ways to choose happiness and fulfillment have seen the benefits.* These truths come from Jesus Christ who loves us unconditionally. They aren't my truths—they're yours and ours as Christ speaks to us through His Word. Some day, I hope we can celebrate our victorious run together.

* Stories in this book of clients and counseling situations are fictionalized accounts that do not depict actual individuals or their experiences.

Exposing Myths

*C*hristian women always have their act together, never experience pain, and live problem-free lives. They always feel that God is close, and they're always kind and loving. They never dislike anyone. Christian women are rarely discouraged, depressed, or confused. Christian women are perfect. Wrong!

These are common myths some Christian women buy into—and some non-Christian women too. I can tell clients over and over again that these myths are not true, but until they're willing to give them up, myths and the craving for some false idea of perfection can and will control them.

Now, let's expose a few more myths to clear our minds for the truth of God's Word to fill us and work through us.

A common myth is that a person can get too spiritual. Some women worry about being overly religious so they bury their Christian life so deep, their own neighbors don't even know they're Christians. On the other hand, some women I meet are afraid of being viewed as *not* spiritual, so they talk a lot *about* God, but they don't talk enough *to* Him.

Some people believe the myth that you'll get into heaven simply because Jesus loves you. But we need a Savior from our sins, not just Jesus' love. God's love was around long before the Cross. The Cross of Jesus Christ gives each person the greatest opportunity of life, for salvation comes from Jesus' sacrificial death on the cross.

Another lie is that all single men and all single women secretly yearn to be married. Not true. Some do, but many are quite content serving God in their singleness and do not desire what God didn't intend.

Another myth is that love is a feeling. *Love is a commitment to action* whether it's toward a mate, a child, a family or church member, or a stranger.

Another myth is that marriage is an equal partnership. In business partnerships that are successful, the partners have given up feeling that it's wrong for one or the other to work harder. So, too, in marriage. One mate may work harder to make the marriage work.

Another myth is that nagging helps husbands and children to change and mature. It never has or will, but many women still give it a try.

Another myth is believing only one Christian church has found the one and only way to Christ. That would mean there would be all Baptists or Methodists or whatever in heaven. No way! No one Christian style of practice based on solid, sound, scriptural doctrine is superior to another. Christ is the One Way. The people in heaven will have come through Christ, and they will love the Lord their God with all their heart, soul, and strength, and their neighbor, too.

How about this myth? Stress comes from outside us when we're in highly pressured situations. Wrong. Stress comes from the way we think about what's going on around us. One person's stress is another person's optimal functioning level.

The truth about believing myths is that they rob us of our joy. And the joy of the Lord is our strength to go on living each day. Life will always have problems. The kingdom of heaven may begin on earth, but it only begins here. This is the space between our prebirth presence of God and our afterdeath presence of God. We need to stop fighting the existence of problems and focus our energies on coping with life as it really is. We can use the tough experiences of real life to grow in our knowledge and love of our Lord.

Let me spell out how dangerous believing myths can be. Some women quit trying to be involved in life at all. Ever wonder why young, lovely, intelligent women commit suicide? Or anorexic women starve themselves? Or women become obsessive-compulsive about their homes or their work? Belief in a myth—a lie—has gripped them, controlled them, and they can no longer function normally, and sometimes no longer function at all.

On the journey of life we will never reach perfection, but we can grow healthy attitudes, practices, and relationships. As we travel through this book together, we'll be looking at healthy, scriptural ways for us as women to cope with real life and keep our promises and commitments to God, ourselves, our families, and our friends.

Exploring Scripture

Rahab (Joshua 2:1–21) wasn't perfect. Deborah (Judges 4:4–14) and Jael (Judges 4:17–22) probably weren't perfect either. Each was God's woman in God's time in God's place and willing to give Him her best. God made good come from it, and He'll do the same for you.

✑ Taking Action

- I bundled many myths together here to get you started thinking about yourself and your life. Make out your own list of myths you actually believe. Discuss with a friend which ones you need to get rid of and why.

- Are there any areas where you're expecting perfection from yourself or others? You are human, after all, and Jesus loves you that way. But prayerfully ask God what you need to do about these unrealistic expectations. And my prayer for you is that as we work through these areas together in this book, God will reveal constructive changes to you.

Lord, it's so easy for myths and lies to slip into my thinking and my feelings. Keep my brain focused on Your Word and Your truth. Free me from believing myths so that each day I grow more and more like You.

৯৯ TWO ৫৯

Representing Christr

hances are if people don't respect the rep, they won't want to do business with the company. In the same way in our various roles, we represent Jesus Christ to the people we meet. If they don't like what they see in us, they may write Christ off their list.

It gives me great joy in this run of life to watch our daughters and daughter-in-law in their roles as representatives of Christ. Along with her primary job of mothering, Tamara is a behind-the-scenes business consultant in her husband's computer software company. She's also an avid tennis player. Wherever she goes, Tamara works to promote family values in her Christian and non-Christian environments. Pamela, a former math teacher, home-schools her three children. She participates in church and community activities and helps others start businesses like her home-based telecommunications business. Kathy is the assistant to the president of a major magazine and helps her husband juggle his career in computer and electronics with doctoral studies at the university. By her example she witnesses with sensitivity and discretion in both her business and social worlds. These are not unusual women, but they are aware of their roles. They desire to represent Christ in everything they do.

So first and foremost in our lives, *nothing* must ever come before Jesus. Husband, job, home, church—we can't allow anything to become a bigger passion in life than Jesus. Our purpose needs to be clear to both ourselves and others. We must keep our primary purpose primary!

Second, Christ values our womanhood and our work. Our talk and our behavior show others that we are aware of our dignity and value and that we place high value on the roles that we play.

Third, we must get into the light. Being a Christian doesn't necessarily mean we are to keep a low profile and stay in the background. "I'm not capable." "It's too much hassle." "What good could it do anyway?" are common excuses we all use to avoid taking authority as God's rep. God is not a God of excuses. We must stand on the basics and speak and act freely with love.

An editor of a secular magazine wondered why Christian women apologized when articles they submitted for publication had biblical values. "Let your work make its own statement," she said. "If it's worth printing, we'll print it." We must not be afraid to bring out spiritual issues, but we need to stay away from religious clichés that the general public doesn't understand.

Fourth, we need to be diligent and leave the results to Him. We need to be like the housewife who took on the challenge of making some important changes in the public school her children attend or the young lawyer who took on a team of seasoned defense lawyers with perseverance and diligence because she knew her cause was right.

And finally, we must pray and let Christ decide where we are to work as His representatives. We must always bathe our involvements in prayer.

📖 Exploring Scripture

We can only be a representative of Christ because we have received authority and empowerment according to Matthew 28:18–20. "All authority has been given to Me in heaven and on earth. Go therefore [because of it] and make disciples of all the nations, baptizing them in the name of the Father and of the Son and of the Holy Spirit, teaching them to observe all things that I have commanded you; and lo, I am with you always, even to the end of the age."

These are some of the most inspirational and encouraging words of Scriptures. Put simply, God's message is, "I'm giving you everything you need to represent me and encourage people to live by my teachings. I'll help you do it; I'll never leave you alone."

Romans 16 illustrates the powerful role of women in the early church. You'll see many wonderful descriptions of female reps there.

In Romans 16:1–2 we read, "I commend to you Phoebe our sister, who is a servant of the church in Cenchrea, that you may receive her in the Lord in a manner worthy of the saints, and assist her in whatever business she has need of you; for indeed she has been a helper of many and of myself also." Obviously Phoebe played a significant part. Remember the early examples recorded in the letters of the apostles were included in Scripture to give us ongoing instruction as to how the church should operate today.

Verse 4 says, "who [Priscilla and Aquila] risked their own necks for my life, to whom not only I give thanks, but also all the churches of the Gentiles." Verse 6 says, "Greet Mary, who labored much for us."

At least seven women are referred to in this chapter. Whenever someone tells us they'd like to represent Christ in society but they don't like the subservient role of Christian women, we need to show them Romans 16 for starters.

✑ Taking Action

- Does your talk and your behavior show others that you're aware of your dignity and value? How can you better project yourself in order to attract others to the Lord?

- Take a moment to write down your various roles. Are you humbly accepting your roles? What good can you accomplish in your environments as God's representative?

- What, if anything, keeps you from exercising your role as God's representative in the world?

Lord, reveal to me through Your Word where and how I can best represent You in my roles as a wife, mom, daughter, friend, volunteer, sister, employer/e, neighbor.

Deepening Friendships

Jesus stripped away surface-level conversation in His social contacts with people. With the Samaritan woman at the well in John 4, He got right to the heart of what was important to her—her marital relationships.

What had she been seeking that was lacking in her life? Jesus knew it was Himself, the Living Water. Her thirsting was related to unquenched desires that nothing on earth could fulfill, and He told her so.

Was the woman at the well surprised at Jesus' talk? Yes! First, because He spoke to her and actually looked at her. How many people had passed this woman by, even shunned her over the years? Jesus didn't seem to care about her past, although He knew all about it. He cared about *her* and what was in her best interests *now*.

Did Jesus and the woman at the well become friends right then and there? For sure. Then she wanted to share Him—the way we all like to introduce our friends to one another—"This is someone I think is special; you will, too, as soon as you get to know each other."

Yes, Jesus' caring was evident, but would He have gotten to know this woman as well if He hadn't identified what was on her heart and what He wanted to do for her? I doubt it. It would have been a pleasant acquaintance, but it wouldn't have been a lasting relationship.

Jesus is a great friend and master communicator. Based on His example, I help my counseling clients identify four different levels of communication. Knowing them can improve your ability to form deep friendships and relate to others. Here are examples of each.

- Level One—Cliché Conversation. "How are you?" "Fine." (There's no real honesty like, "I'm having a bad day" or "I feel great because . . .")

- Level Two—Reporting Facts. "I have a cold." "It's raining hard."

- Level Three—Ideas or Judgments. "Everybody should take vitamins." "It's lucky I brought my umbrella."

- Level Four—Feelings or Emotions. "I'm disappointed I can't go skiing." "The rain always makes me feel a little down."

Why is Kathie Lee such a popular talk show hostess? She's willing to be herself, to talk about her failings, to discuss personal things like shaving her legs. She cries when she's moved, and she can laugh at herself and others. She can tease, and she tempers her serious comments with levity. Her entire audience feels like she's interacting with them at Level Four.

My daughter Pam has become close friends with the woman who delivers her mail by asking how her day is going, just as Jesus asked the woman at the well and then listened with caring.

My friend Pat is a "Level Four" friend. She always wants to know how I really am. And in turn she tells me her dreams and dilemmas. She shares her deepest self in a thousand ways. Because our communication is intimate, Pat knows when I have a physical or emotional or spiritual need, and she's eager to help.

When we moved to a large house twenty years ago, Pat found extra furniture for us. We still use the kitchen table! When we went to Europe recently, she and her husband, Tom, veteran travelers, outlined a tour for us. When our son was hospitalized in another city, Pat came to spend a few days and pray with me. When our daughter Pam married, Pat decorated the church, and she and her daughter Caryl made the bridesmaids' bouquets. I am incredibly blessed by Pat and several other wonderful friends God has put into my life.

Meaningful friendships develop by going past communication Levels One, Two and Three. This doesn't mean we share our deepest feelings with every person we meet. Like Jesus we must pray for the Father's wisdom. But it is important that those we come in contact with sense we're open to Level Four communication. Keep striving for open and honest conversations.

Exploring Scripture

What we say and how we say it affects our friendships. What can we learn from these Scriptures?

- Proverbs 27:2—"Let another man praise you, not your own mouth."
- Ecclesiastes 5:3b—"And a fool's voice is known by his many words."
- Ephesians 4:29—"Do not let any unwholesome talk come out of your mouths, but only what is helpful for building others up according to other needs, that it may benefit those who listen" (NIV).

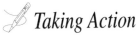 *Taking Action*

- Which of the four levels of communication are you most comfortable at now?

- What are some ways you can go to a deeper level?

- Are there some women in your life you'd like as closer friends? Write their names here.

Arrange to meet these women for lunch or coffee and practice developing your communication skills. It's OK to tell these friends how you'd like to deepen your friendship with them and work on your relational skills. That's being open.

❦

Lord, lead me to the friends who will minister in my life and for whom I can be a true Christian sister.

༖ FOUR ༀ

Ditching Demons

*D*emons are mentioned often in the New Testament, but we don't hear demons talked about much today. Ever wonder where they've all gone? Have demons become extinct like dinosaurs? I wish!

The existence of demons can be scary. Many women, including me, would prefer to forget about them, but that's not what Jesus did. He recognized the presence of demons and dealt with them.

Demons have not stopped their powerful, destructive work. If we're having any kind of turmoil in our homes, we need to check to see if we've given an opportunity for the Devil to enter. We must get rid of games, music, magazines, books, TV programs, ornaments, or decorations that could serve as doorways into our spirits or the spirit of any member of our families. We have full authority in the name of Jesus to calmly order demons to take off.

Ouija boards, horoscopes, occult-related computer games, music, and rituals are often experimented with at parties our children may attend. We need to openly discuss these spiritual dangers with them, just as we discuss their physical safety. Anything connected with the occult or witchcraft is destructive and must be avoided.

I counseled a fourteen-year-old boy with green hair. He had a history of drug use in junior high school in Florida. He had come to Wisconsin from Florida to live with his grandmother in a Christian home. He said he wanted to get his act together and agreed to live by his grandmother's rules, but he violated them over and over. Each time he disobeyed he sounded genuinely sorry, but he'd soon repeat the offense. During our counseling sessions, I discovered he'd brought his satanic rock music, pictures, and occult jewelry with him to his grandmother's house. When he got rid of these connections to his satanic past, his rebellion stopped.

The fourth-grade daughter of a young mom I counseled ran away from home several times. The police found the girl each time, and she willingly returned. During counseling the mom revealed the girl had a computer game with witches and sorcerers in which the main character always died. The girl enjoyed the game. One day, to the mother's amazement, the daughter shoved the computer game into her closet and said she hated it. Almost immediately the girl's disposition changed dramatically for the better. Several days later, the daughter felt compelled to take the game out again. The mom didn't object. As soon as the girl began playing the game, her out-of-control behavior resumed. The mom refused to believe my suggestion that her daughter's behavior and the game were connected. She was afraid of her daughter's reaction if she got rid of the game permanently. The see-saw continued. Can we say these behavioral changes are only coincidence?

In counseling there are definitely times when I can identify a perverse, demonic resistance in a client who knows what to do to be free but refuses to comply.

Satan is a subtle, slippery spirit with other weapons that can fool us. One of his most effective weapons is to toss accusations at us and fill us with self-doubt. Put-downs and mockery are his specialty. Ever hear anything like this: "You're too loud" (or "too quiet" or "too pushy" or "not assertive enough" or "not qualified" or "not capable"), "You sure messed up that situation, dummy," or "You shouldn't have gotten involved"?

Another wily trick we must watch out for is a grumbling spirit. We can identify it when we talk to ourselves in words like "I'm always left to handle all the details" or "Just once, I wish I didn't have to do this."

Warning! We need to guard against developing "demon mania" and dumping everything on demons. There are three sources of temptation: the world, the flesh, and the Devil—not just the Devil. In times past some people went to extremes and found a demon everywhere. C. S. Lewis sums up the right attitude toward evil spirits in his classic book, *The Screwtape Letters*. He claims the two biggest dangers regarding Satan are focusing on the Devil too much and ignoring the Devil's existence entirely which is equally harmful. We need to learn the facts about these wily spirits.

Exploring Scripture

- Mark 1:39: "And He was preaching in their synagogues throughout all Galilee, and casting out demons." Demons are quite common.
- Mark 5: 3–4: "This man lived in the tombs, and no one could bind him any more, not even with a chain. For he had often been chained hand and foot, but he tore the chains apart and broke the irons on his feet. No one was strong enough to subdue him" (NIV). Demons can create unnatural physical strength.
- Mark 5:5: "Night and day among the tombs and in the hills he would cry out and cut himself with stones" (NIV). Demons can make people cut themselves or otherwise harm their bodies, but they must respond to Jesus.

- Mark 7:29–30: "Then he told her, 'For such a reply, you may go; the demon has left your daughter'" (NIV). Demons can enter children.
- Mark 5: 6–7: "When he saw Jesus from a distance, he ran and fell on his knees in front of him. He shouted at the top of his voice, 'What do you want with me, Jesus, Son of the Most High God? Swear to God that you won't torture me!'" (NIV). They sure knew Jesus!

Think of demons as you would a spiritual germ. Annihilate it! They may be around, but Jesus has given us effective control. We must decide that no big ugly germ is going to get near us or our family. If you come in contact with a demon, remember the Word of God in Luke 10:17b, "Lord, even the demons submit to us in your name" (NIV). Second Thessalonians 3:3 reads, "But the Lord is faithful, and he will strengthen and protect you from the evil one" (NIV).

Taking Action

Take preventive measures. The technique for identifying counterfeit money is to study the real thing. Fill your own and your children's minds and hearts with the truth about Jesus and with wholesome activities, thoughts, words, and media experiences.

Jesus deals with demons forcefully but not harshly. In Mark 5:12–13 we read, "The demons begged Jesus, 'Send us among the pigs; allow us to go into them'" (NIV). Notice when the unclean spirits entered the swine, the swine destroyed themselves. Demonic involvement in our children can lead to their self-destruction.

Teach your children 1) the Devil is real and 2) to resist the Devil, and he will take off.

Another way to give an "in" to the Devil is through anger and discord with others. Ephesians 4:26–27 says, "Never go to bed angry—don't give the devil that sort of foothold" (PHILLIPS).

- How can we apply these words daily?

✦

Lord, show me any foothold that Satan has in my life and home. Give me strength to resist Satan. Thank You for Your protection and for making Satan flee from me.

Ordering Your World

M y friend Kathy keeps both a giveaway bag in her closet for possessions her family no longer needs and a clutter bag on her kitchen counter for emotional garbage she needs to discard. The clutter bag reminds her every day to keep throwing away inappropriate feelings of jealousy, anger, desire for revenge toward people who've hurt her, disappointments, and so on. She's a sweet, godly lady because she doesn't let her "junk" get out of order.

Clutter is the opposite of order. To clutter means to litter or pile in a disordered state. Clutter isn't just an accumulation of papers and odd socks; it can also be an accumulation of thoughts, ideas, and emotional feelings. Clutter is bad because it chokes and kills order and beauty. We want to keep our heads, hearts, and hands clutter-free.

Disordered emotional feelings and thoughts make it harder for us to maintain physical order. Did you ever notice how hard it is to keep our homes organized when we're emotionally upset? Or how living in a mess of physical disorder all around us makes it harder to keep our thoughts and feelings orderly? Clutter creates a vicious cycle.

If clutter and disorder have taken over your home and your life, how do you clean up? You can examine with a ruthless eye whatever needs reordering and then eliminate anything that's not 1) essential, 2) healthy, 3) productive, or 4) fun.

Let's start with feelings. What feelings cause you to collect more possessions than you need or can use? Insecurity? Anger at a husband who doesn't meet your emotional needs? Do you punish him by running up your charge cards? Do you live in fear of a future shortfall? Throw this emotional garbage away.

Maybe you're caught in a chain of inherited physical clutter—too much junk! Your mom was a collector and now so are you. All that stuff must be sorted through and the excess removed regularly. Should you save the last inch of paint because you might need it someday? If you do need it again, chances are you won't be able to find it or it'll have dried up. Can't God provide paint again? Wouldn't He prefer to help you find the right paint than have you accumulate "stuff"?

Perhaps the words "waste not, want not" were drummed into you.

They aren't in the Bible, you know. "Give, and it will be given to you" is written in God's Word (Luke 6:38).

Sometimes things aren't in order because no one has thought of a good place to put them, or they think keeping things in order requires too much work. Actually, order saves more time and makes life easier later.

How about activities? Is your daily life too cluttered? Are there a thousand good things you could do each day, many work opportunities, all kinds of choices for the way you and your family spend your time? Ask God for wisdom in choosing what's best. Draw up a plan. Every household I've ever visited runs better when the members follow a routine that sets the structure for each day, each week, and each month.

How many new schedules or new routines for organization have you started only to have each fall by the wayside within a week or two, maybe even days or hours? Your reordered schedule needs to be flexible, fun, and beneficial in order to give you the motivation to stick to it. Remember, moms, you are usually the hub of the scheduling activity that goes on in a household.

One of my client's favorite phrases was "I've got to get my family on a good schedule," as if a plan is a living creation that could manage her household for her. My client tried dozens of schedules before she came to me. She'd go through a period of discouragement and then start the cycle again: new plan, start, stop, new plan, start, stop.

My suggestion to her: *keep life simple.* Plan in terms of priorities: God, family, work, friends. Based on giving time to these four areas, evaluate your schedule three times a year during the major change times of your family life:

1. At the start of the school year
2. In January when school starts up after Christmas
3. In June when school lets out

If you're single or married without children, evaluate September 1, January 1, and June 1. Consider mealtime, bedtime, chore expectations, and general life changes. For example, yard clean-up goes on the June chart, snow removal on the January chart. Have at least one meal a day as a family—breakfast or dinner. Decide with your husband how strictly you want to enforce your rules. Explain your decision to your children and remind them often of the consequences of disobedience.

Children often start each day by getting dressed and finding their things for school. That's second-best. Start them with a morning prayer as soon as they get out of bed or at breakfast before they leave: "God, please order our thoughts, our activities, and our things. Bless and protect us and bless others through us."

Tell a close friend about your decision to keep every area in your life—including your schedule—free from clutter. Have a "clutter check" with someone once a week.

 Exploring Scripture

Read Genesis 1:4–10. Notice how God divided light from darkness and then labeled what He did. How's that for organization?

Next God took time to review His work and "saw that it was good." Taking time to feel satisfaction from what you've accomplished stimulates you to continue projects.

Taking Action

- Make a list of the areas in your home that need to be "uncluttered."

- What activities can you eliminate from your schedule?

Lord, reveal any disorder in my life that has come from thoughts and feelings like envy, bitterness, or guilt. Please help me remove the clutter of too many possessions and too many activities.

Staying Calm, Cheerful, and Consistent

Do you ever get caught in the swirl and whirl of life? I do. It happens when it's dinner time, and I've rushed to the store for something, and I'm scheduled back in my office for a 7:30 appointment. Even as I berate myself for doing too much in too short a time, I feel myself becoming tense.

When the game, the deal, the family concern is on the line, tension becomes a vibrating sensation. Then it's time for the CCC Plan. It's always effective, but you have to remember to use it. CCC stands for staying **CALM, CHEERFUL, AND CONSISTENT.**

When we choose to be calm, cheerful, and consistent with our Christian beliefs, we don't say or do things we'll regret later. The circumstances don't change, but we stay focused in our thoughts and actions which makes all the difference! We keep operating in a straight line instead of functioning in circular fashion and ending up completely flustered and right back where we started.

The CCC Plan is especially important in disciplining children. A client used to have to be furious before she'd correct or spank her child. By then she'd already lost control and started yelling. When she learned to stay calm, cheerful, and act consistently with her beliefs about children's proper behavior, the whole atmosphere of her home became more pleasant.

Exploring Scripture

Is this all just psychobabble? No, the principle is as old as the Bible. Jesus taught the CCC Plan, and He always modeled it. Take the storm on the Sea of Galilee when the frantic apostles awakened Jesus. He could have jumped up and said, "Oh no, what are we going to do now?" Jesus stayed cheerful and calm. Jesus knew He could stop the storm, and we need to remember that He can stop our storms too. And what a model of calmness, cheerfulness, and consistency we have in Jesus in

John 1:14–22! Even in His anger when He cleansed the temple, He showed control and turned the act into a lesson for His disciples. Look for other incidents in the Gospels that reveal Jesus showing CCC.

✎ Taking Action

Here are some tips for staying calm, cheerful, and consistent over the small stuff (that's what creates most of your emotional stress):

1. When you feel flustered, often your natural inclination is to rush ahead in your thoughts and movements. Instead, start to move and speak in slow motion. You can regain mastery by being CCC.
2. You can calm or cheer yourself in seconds when you pray. Focusing on Jesus and eternity can relax you. What you're doing at the moment takes on a different perspective.
3. Think about something pleasant, relaxing, or rewarding that you've done or are going to do—a cup of tea, where you're going next month, a cozy time to read a book.
4. Picture yourself acting calm, cheerful, and consistent. Acting "as if" truly helps your body focus on becoming what you portray. Act brave, graceful, and determined.
5. If cooperating with the inevitable is your only choice, do it with CCC like an heir of God. CCC comes from knowing He has ultimate control.

Preserve your emotional energy. You can't be casual about an overwhelming problem like a sick child or a company take-over that's threatening your job. But, even then, don't drain your precious emotional reserves with hysteria.

- When are you most challenged to remain calm, cheerful, and consistent?

- Which of the suggested behaviors might work for you?

- Record how you'll apply them this week.

Lord, thank You that I can first come to You in prayer when my life becomes frenzied and chaotic. Thank You for modeling calm, cheerful, and consistent behavior in the storms of life. I want Your Spirit to fill me; I want to be like You.

Decorating Your Temples

We women have two temples to decorate—the personal temple of our soul and body, which is occupied by the Holy Spirit, and the temple that is our home. We'll talk about our homes now, and our bodies and souls in "Keeping Body and Soul Fit" (16).

We're all interested in having an attractive home. God created beauty upon earth as recorded in Genesis. Later, when a temple, an earthly dwelling, was to be built for God, He cared about every minute detail and made sure it was decorated according to His specifications. Picky, picky! Yes! So are we women in our innate desire to have a comfortable nest for ourselves and our families.

Occasionally we hear a phrase like "a Christian shouldn't be interested in material possessions." But it's OK to appreciate nice things. Man's first home was awesome, the Garden of Eden, and our future home is heaven. It's all right to enhance our surroundings as long as it's not causing us to be stingy with God or other people. Many women (and men) have trouble seeing God at all unless they're living in a visually pleasant, organized setting. Notice I didn't say expensive. You can have a lovely home on a tiny budget. Here are some suggestions.

Often what a home needs more than anything else is simply a creative reorganization. A messy home is never attractive. Maybe you need to establish a different plan for maintaining order. (See 5, "Ordering Your World.")

Instead of adding more things, we often just need to streamline and give space to our favorite possessions. Learn to be creative with the furnishings you have. Design some cozy sitting areas in the living room or kitchen. Try angling your furniture diagonally across corners. Add new things gradually.

Shopping for second-hand furniture is a wonderful way to refurbish a house one item at a time. I happen to like the style and design of older furniture, so much of my furniture comes from used furniture shops. These pieces have character and interesting stories to tell, and the price is often reasonable. Our daughter-in-law found a gorgeous floral chintz sofa at the Salvation Army for a fifth of its cost new.

I pray over anything I bring into our home—for the people who made it, for those who used it before me (if it's not new), and for my family to be blessed by our temporary ownership. (Everything we own is only ours temporarily.)

Check out magazines and catalogs at the library for ideas. A friend of mine makes stunning slipcovers and drapes from sheets. She uses hidden cup hooks and rubber bands to hang the drapes. With T-pins she holds the fabric in place on her furniture covers. Now she has a thriving small business.

If it's a reasonable expectation, do what needs doing yourself, and you'll receive creative satisfaction as well as save money on your projects. Painting wood furniture or stripping, staining, and varnishing a painted piece is like getting a brand-new piece of furniture! Don't get carried away with a Do-It-Yourself project, though, for it can cost more than it's worth—especially if it creates emotional distress and frustration in you. And D.I.Y. is not always cheaper. Factor in your time as well as your talent.

If you're not talented in this area, ask your friends, including friends who go to other churches, where you can find someone you might hire reasonably to help you redecorate.

Helping one another can be the most fun way to redecorate. How about a progressive closet cleaning? Ladies from church or a fellowship group can move from house to house and clean one person's closets per week, or they can go to three or four homes in one day and clean one closet at each house. (Yes, this takes humility.) Share your resources and your talents.

Once a month a Baptist church in Florida offers a decorating day for anyone in the church who requests help. Women bring their sewing machines, donated curtains, glue, paintbrushes, hammers, and nails. The homemaker shares in advance where she would most like help. One room or perhaps the entire house may need to be redone. Everyone brings a bag lunch. The women visit as they work and enjoy decorating one another's homes.

Other group projects might include planting flower or vegetable gardens in spring and sharing perennials by thinning and dividing them. These "day-outs" are so much fun and also inexpensive. Many hands and heads work more efficiently.

A word of caution: Don't get too much of your ego tied into your house. That's dangerous. Fabrics and furniture wear; styles change. Jesus is the same yesterday, today, and forever, and He makes all things new. He's the only safe spot for a woman's ego.

 *Exploring Scripture*

Read 2 Chronicles 3 to see how precisely the temple in Jerusalem was built and decorated. The temple was created according to God's exact specifications as precisely as humans could build because the building was an act of worship in itself. The temple was to be used for worshipers sacrificing offerings to God.

Everything about us is a living sacrifice to God. God wants us to make our homes as lovely as we possibly can—whether we live in a hut, a motor home, or an estate.

 Taking Action

- What homemaking talent do you have that you could share with the other women in your church?

- Look around your home with a critical eye. What does it need? More color, texture, design? Would a transformation with sheets, rubber bands, and T-pins help?

Lord, help me to make the temple of my home as attractive as possible. Help me to use the things I have to their best advantage and to be gracious in accepting the good ideas of my friends. Help me to be generous in helping others in the areas I do well.

EIGHT

Growing in Love

The Knotts, a prominent political couple who lived in Tallahassee, Florida, were married over seventy years. They died within eight days of each other. He was 101; she was 93. After all those years, they couldn't be separated more than a week!

A friend of mine describes her marriage, "After thirty years my husband and I almost don't need words to communicate. He knows what I'm thinking and I know what he's thinking. We still talk, because we like the sound of each other's voice. But," she adds, "the first ten years of our marriage I would have traded in my husband many times if my circumstances would have allowed it. Now I can't imagine life without him."

Looking back I, too, consider it a miracle of the grace of God that my husband and I survived the first ten years of our marriage. I wanted to have the perfect marriage. This desire wasn't a great blessing but a great cause of confusion and discord. As two strong-willed, independent people accustomed to pleasing ourselves, we were in for a shock and at times great pain.

The second week of marriage we had a horrible argument over my husband's socks—I had lost some in the wash and became as defensive as a bull when he demanded I be more careful. I didn't sleep all night, sure that I'd married a hypercritical tyrant— definitely the wrong man. Over those first months I often asked God if our union was a mistake.

I admit now I wasn't Mrs. Perfection, but then I didn't know how many faults I had. There were more downs than ups as God grew my husband and me wiser in Him and made strong and beautiful bonds out of our inadequacies. What a thrill to experience God's changes!

Problems increased when I felt as if I hadn't done enough or when my husband took advantage and abused my helpful quality. Sometimes I stepped in and did things that I should have let my husband do. Sometimes I didn't do things I should have done. It took many years to work out the right balance in our work, our parenting, and our ministry.

At times my husband still frustrates me, and I annoy him when we both see a situation from totally different views. We've been married over thirty years, and he still does things that are incomprehensible to me. But most often, miraculously at times, we are completely like-minded.

Most of the women I counsel have wondered about their marriages at some time or other. I'm convinced most people choose to marry someone who is like-minded in values but different in personality. They agree about most things, but not about everything. (There can be no interrelationship between two entities that are identical.) But when the differences of temperament pop out between two people, the differences can seem to overshadow the similarities.

Do you ever feel like bailing out? Remember, this isn't a seven-year contract you promised. Marriage is for a lifetime—not of sameness but mutual change for the better. You were created by God to be a helper. Desiring to please and help your husband is an ingrained characteristic.

A smooth marital relationship is easier, of course, if you married a Christian man or a man with personal integrity. But maybe you didn't. It's easy to lose your respect for your husband if he acts unethically. However, God doesn't lose respect for your husband's personhood. God appreciates your husband even when He sees behavior that He despises. He remains committed, and He expects you to do the same.*

📖 *Exploring Scripture*

Read what real love for your spouse is like in Song of Songs 8:6–7: "Place me like a seal over your heart, like a seal on your arm; for love is as strong as death, its jealousy unyielding as the grave. It burns like blazing fire, like a mighty flame. Many waters cannot quench love; rivers cannot wash it away. If one were to give all the wealth of his house for love, it would be utterly scorned" (NIV).

- Love can be genuine or superficial. What kind of love is Solomon describing here?

- Read Psalm 26, "The Prayer of a Good Man," and pray this psalm may be true for your husband.

✎ Taking Action

- My "3-3 Tip"—What is there to appreciate about your spouse right now? Make a list of three things you appreciate about him, tell him what they are, and remind yourself of them three times a day.

- The most powerful (and often overlooked) way you can be a helper is to pray for your husband. A man can be protected from temptations if he has a wife who prays for his protection. Pray this for thirty days and see what happens. Write down three specific areas you will pray about.

*Lord, give my husband wisdom in every decision,
big and little. Help him grow in character qualities pleasing to
You, Lord. Use him directly or indirectly to further Your
kingdom. Shelter him from any harm—
physical, emotional, or spiritual.*

---

* If your husband isn't a Christian, read *Unbelieving Husbands and the Wives Who Love Them* by Michael Fanstone (Vine Books, 1996). It's realistic and encouraging.

Respecting Your Mate

*D*uring counseling sessions, I often hear a woman using put-downs about her husband's shortcomings. I can only guess how she must talk at home!

If somebody nags us or yells at us, we feel demeaned, disrespected, and put down, and so do our husbands! God never yells or nags. We need to remember that when we speak to our husbands. It can take a long time to restore emotional intimacy after we've yelled or made sarcastic or callous comments to our mate. We must make a point to never dump our crabbiness or disappointment on our husbands. We can maintain the passion in our marriages with tender words, kindness, and loving, physical intimacy.

Over the years through my counseling experiences I've collected ideas about respecting and loving our husbands. Here's my list.

Ten Ways to Show Respect and Love for Your Husband
That Can Keep You Out of Counseling!

1. Give up the bad memories . For whatever reasons you're harboring resentment, ask God to enable you to drop it. Harboring resentment makes us overly sensitive and subtly hostile.

2. Be polite at all times. A Hungarian woman married fifty years claims there's seldom been a harsh word between her and her husband. Unrealistic? My friend said, "You don't really believe that!" I do. It takes a lot of effort, but it's worth it!

3. Avoid complaints—subtly implied or spoken aloud. Spouses have sensitive antennas. No sniping, sarcasm, name-calling, or other rudeness. And never tell your children negative things about their father!

4. Blend your interests with your husband's so that you can have more time together. If he loves to fish and you don't, maybe you'd

enjoy sitting in the boat reading. Do more of what brings you closer and less of what doesn't.

5. Make time for love. Most problems arise from being too busy or too tired. Overscheduling your life elsewhere makes it hard to keep special dates for lovemaking. There's nothing wrong with love appointments—you enjoyed dates when you courted!

6. Be militant about having a good relationship and not letting anyone or anything interfere with it—not even parents, in-laws, children, brothers, sisters. Show your husband that you respect his opinions, his feelings, his desires. Expect some bumps, but be solution-oriented when there's a difficulty.

7. Surprise him. Do the unexpected. Try a kiss instead of a grumble, even if you're in a situation where grumbling seems right. You'll find you get what you give. He may start surprising you.

8. Stay away from people who help feed negativity about your spouse. Share any problem very discreetly outside the relationship. Avoid "spouse attack."

9. Never forget that divorce doesn't solve the problems you think it will; it creates different ones and hurts children whatever their age. Find causes and explanations for your husband's behavior. See him as a unique individual and listen to his point of view.

10. Your husband chose you and you him. Be loyal to the commitment you made. Shine the light on yourself and find ways you can both grow into a mature couple.

Exploring Scripture

Here are several Scriptures that are powerhouse verses for relationships:

- "A gentle answer turns away wrath" (Proverbs 15:1 NIV).

- "Refrain from anger and turn from wrath; do not fret—it leads only to evil" (Psalm 37:8 NIV).

✎ Taking Action

- Praise your husband in front of your child or children. Make him a "Great Husband" or "Father of the Year" certificate and hang it on the refrigerator where everyone will see it.

- Ask him what you can do to improve your relationship with him. Write it down and remember to do it each week.

- Think of any ways you tend to "put down" your husband. What positive terms can you use to replace negative comments?

❧❧❧

Lord, please help me to see the good things about my husband and to remember to praise him for those qualities. Increase my loyalty and help me to choose friends who will help and not hurt our marriage. Quiet my complaining spirit, and may I surprise him with love.

TEN

Trusting God

*W*hen we're really down or going through an incredibly tough time, can we believe God is at work, even in the mess or devastation we see?

Greg and Gail's nine-year-old daughter was killed in a car accident months after the girl had received Christ and brought her entire family to the Lord. Gail's prayer the day after the accident was that somehow God would use this terrible tragedy for good. She wrote a letter to pass out at her daughter's funeral, which was also published in the local paper, describing how her daughter had led the family to Christ and how she knew her daughter was in heaven with Jesus.

Still, the loss was almost more than their family could bear. It was the darkest, most difficult period of their lives. The hole left by their daughter's death will fill a little over the years, but it will never fill completely because a child is always part of the family. Gail and Greg are praying now about how to direct their extra time and energy.

The accident that claimed her daughter's life was out of anyone's control, and Gail realized it wasn't right to blame God for what happened. In other situations, however, I've observed that clients struggle to trust God because deep down in their hearts, they do blame Him. They believe an all-powerful God should be able to divert any difficulty.

Marietta, a single mom with two boys aged ten and seven, admits (although reluctantly) that maybe she did divorce her husband too hastily and for selfish reasons. Now he's remarried and has more children. She's struggling financially to raise her sons. As Marietta leans on God, she's discovering He will help her through these times even if she may have brought her afflictions and difficulties upon herself.

Fortunately, God's love and mercy do not depend on never making mistakes. We must never despair when for a time things seem to get worse instead of better. We must remember that Creation and the culminating work of the Cross at Calvary occurred during visible darkness.

Never, ever does God ignore our cries for help, no matter how dark our circumstances appear.

Exploring Scripture

When we're going through a time when trusting is difficult, we can meditate on God's Word to us.

"Shout for joy, O heavens; rejoice, O earth; burst into song, O mountains! For the LORD comforts his people and will have compassion on his afflicted ones" (Isaiah 49:13 NIV).

We can trust God when we or someone we love is sick.

"O LORD my God, I called to you for help and you healed me. O LORD, you brought me up from the grave; you spared me from going down into the pit" (Psalm 30:2 NIV).

Sometimes someone we love has been sick and then healed and has had a wonderful, fruitful extended life for years. Later, illness returns and our loved one dies. Will we still trust in God's plan?

Can we grieve like King David did for his son? He fasted and prayed and wouldn't stop while his son's life was in danger. But as soon as his son died, David got up and went about his business. Did King David still carry grief and sorrow for his son who was no longer with him? Of course. But King David knew his role as an intercessor was over and that God would want David to trust his son to Him and get on with God's purpose for King David's own life.

Taking Action

• Who or what are your sources of security? Are they trustworthy?

• What do you need to trust God with right now?

⚜

Dear Lord, help me to trust You through all the hard times of life—the things I do not understand and the hard things I know I could have prevented. Help me to put the past behind, growing in Your love and seeking Your purposes for me day by day.

ELEVEN

Praying Well

eth knows she should pray more, and she means to. When she tries, it's sort of vague. She wonders when, why, and how to do it.

Can we become holy without talking with God? Can we become scuba divers without showing up for instruction? Hardly! The presence of God is the milieu, the environment in which our holiness is created and developed. That's how the holy people in the Bible got close to God—by conversing with Him.

Over years of seeing God work repeatedly in response to her prayers, a friend of mine now says about everything, "I've got to pray about this." Whether it's a realtor wanting to list her house or it's deciding where to go for a vacation, she's developed the habit of asking God His plans for her before she does anything.

Another friend, who has a job in a challenging nursing home setting, asks God to ordain her hands and her steps every time she enters the building. She prays, "May I give out the right medications to each of my patients and perform my many nursing tasks correctly."

We can pray about anything! My prayer for the garden in the woods around our house is that it resemble just a bit of the Garden of Eden and that God is honored there with no disobedience. A peculiar thing to ask for, but why not?

What is prayer anyway? Prayer is the link in the God-us relationship. Relationships require conversation. Some people like to talk to God out loud so they go for a walk or talk to God when they're in the car.

Who should we pray for? All those in our family and our circle of friends, as well as the people we meet as we move through the day. While I wait in check-out lines at stores, I often pray for the clerk or the person next to me in line.

How should we pray? How about Paul's prayer: "For this reason we also, since the day we heard it, do not cease to pray for you, and to ask that you may be filled with the knowledge of His will in all wisdom and spiritual understanding; that you may walk worthy of the Lord, fully pleasing Him, being fruitful in every good work and increasing in the knowlege of God" (Colossians 1:9–10).

If we want to learn how to pray well, we need to study people like Hannah, a childless woman in the Old Testament. She made a desperate plea for a child and surrendered her life to God (1 Samuel 1:10). Esther is another great example of a woman who knew the value of prayer. She asked others to fast and pray for her before she would go in and approach the King (Esther 4:16).

What should we pray for? Hezekiah made a request for an extended life and God honored it. There's nothing wrong with asking for specific needs.

Prayer is not a speech contest. David said simply and sincerely what was on his heart. He didn't edit himself to try to say nice things. He told God when he was frantic, joyful, fearful, angry. Paul's communication with God was different. He threaded his words with praise.

Our words need to be genuine and sincere. Short prayers are OK. A short prayer forces us to focus in on the main message. Short and specific is great—so is long and detailed.

When should we pray? Always, all days. Prayer is the intimate whispering of our hearts and our listening for His intimate answer. Today I prayed before I cleaned my closet, "Lord help me get rid of these clothes I don't need and simplify my wardrobe." Then I went in there and held up each item of clothing one by one and prayed, "Do you want to see me in this, Lord, yes or no? Is there someone I should give this to?" While I was doing this sorting, I looked at my watch and saw it was ten o'clock, and a young girl had asked me to pray for her test today. "Keep her calm, please, Lord," I prayed.

How often do we need to bring our own family's needs to God? Daily. We send our children out with coats and mittens in the winter, rainwear in the spring, and sunscreen in the summer to protect them physically. But do we sometimes forget their spiritual and emotional protection? We can pray, "Lord, please send ministering angels to surround, guide and protect my child today. Thank You for hearing my prayer."

Exploring Scripture

"Then He spoke a parable to them, that men always ought to pray and not lose heart" (Luke 18:1). Jesus told about the widow who kept after a judge to help her get justice until the judge finally agreed to help. We can't expect instant answers as if God is a divine drive-through. But we do know that the minute we pray, we release supernatural power into a situation and that we will eventually see the fruits of our prayers.

✎ Taking Action

There's nothing more powerful we can do for those we love than regularly pray for them. Will you make a commitment to be a daily prayer warrior for the needs of others God puts into your life? Start a prayer notebook now. List people and their needs. Next to each name write a short sentence about specifically what you're asking God to do now.

- List the people who need prayer and the situations you need to pray about.

Lord, I need to pray continually; I need to bathe my very life in prayer. Help me to think first to pray, linking You into every thought and event and person of my life. Thank You that You hear and love and answer.

Playing Like a Child

Do we see like a child sees, feel like a child feels? We can spend time with children to learn to enjoy things like watching a faucet turn or a breeze blow, smelling grass freely washed by rain, and feeling soap slip through our fingers. All the ordinary things become extraordinary when we stop to appreciate them like a child.

When we use all of our senses to touch, taste, smell, hear, see everything around us, like touching the wings of a butterfly or the smoothness of a pen or capturing the scent of evergreen needles in a little box to remember Christmas in March, we give ourselves the gift of wondering and pretending with our children. We experience these joys *with* them, and for a moment we can lay aside our directing and problem solving.

Why did Jesus want the little children to come near Him? Surely He delighted in their presence. We all should. Children are wise in many ways. They savor experiences rather than speeding through them. Children who haven't been overscheduled in too many activities move with a smooth innate rhythm. We can learn from them.

Jane's children grew up around her like unappreciated wildflowers. Jane never took time to laugh and play with her children. One day she heard a lecture on humor and realized there wasn't enough laughter in her family's life. She decided to try to tell silly stories and develop private jokes to share with each of her children. Her children had never heard her laughing except at the movies. Although her children were adolescents by then, they loved her efforts. Jane was amazed at the warmth and joy that humor added to their family's life. Such a simple thing, but Jane had never tried it before.

📖 Exploring Scripture

I imagine Jesus and His disciples shared some great fun and private jokes. In Psalm 126:2 we read about laughter, "Then our mouth was filled with laughter, and our tongue with singing. Then said they among the nations, 'The LORD has done great things for them.'"

That's true today, too. The Lord has done great things, so let's laugh and enjoy!

✎ Taking Action

Take lots of breaks to have fun with your husband, children, and friends. Plan and prepare activities, but always leave a margin for God to map in His changes. Make a commitment to spend at least a half hour a day being unhurried. It will give you time to play.

- List the things you can do to add more joy and laughter to your home life. Visit the library for joke books? Story books? Watch a GOOD cartoon with your child and try to see it through his or her eyes? Just start making a little time to play, and see the differences it makes. PLAY!!

Lord, how You loved children, and I so desire to be childlike in my trust of You and in my enjoyment of the delights of life. Help me to hear the humor, enjoy the pleasures, relish the music and rhythm of life!

☙ THIRTEEN ❧

Choosing Ministry

I told a Christian client who wanted more structure and purpose in her efforts for the Lord, "You already are a minister, you know." She answered, "No way!"

Ministry is simply the way we bring glory to God through the course of our lives. If we're a daughter, a wife, a mother, an employer, or an employee, we have a major ministry! How do we best glorify God in our very important roles and in the world beyond?

God's given us a huge clue! When we stop to examine ourselves, we know! Let me explain. I'm a terrible singer; I once considered taking voice lessons to improve my singing—mostly so I would be comfortable in church situations that involved group singing. My motive was pride, not pleasing God and serving others. I don't know why God didn't gift me with a singing voice, but I do know He gave me other interests and strengths in the areas of counseling and writing to use on behalf of others.

So when we examine ourselves, we must look first at our motives for ministry. Then we look at our strengths and our areas of interest. Is our purpose in seeking ministry opportunities merely to expand the church, please others, or receive personal praise? Or simply to help out because someone has to do it? Or is our motive to glorify God? That's the only motive worth our time and energy.

Caring for the unborn, the sick, those in prison, the poor, the parentless children—thousands of formal and informal ministries exist to meet these needs, but more help is always needed. Some women have a powerful ministry providing the one home in the neighborhood where children can come after school to enjoy the presence of a caring mom. Many spontaneous neighborhood Bible studies have arisen like this—both among the children and among the parents who have seen the love and care extended to their children.

The very fact that more help in the "harvest" is *always* needed, however, calls for a word of caution. A young woman named Jenna came in to see me, a dedicated Christian who also suffered from bulimia. She tended to say *yes* to every ministry-related task in her church that someone asked her to do. In reality Jenna couldn't handle all the "I'll do its" that she allowed into her life and as a result would become depressed. Eventually she'd grow so frustrated she'd bow out of everything. But soon she'd start over and become just as packed with commitments again.

Jenna finally saw the relationship between eating too much food then purging and overcommitting to responsibilities then purging activities at church. As so often happens, our bodies tell the real story. Though our emotions and our wills can place impossible demands on us physically, sooner or later our bodies will rebel. (This example doesn't mean every person who has bulimia overextends her commitments at church or elsewhere; this was simply Jenna's problem.)

Jenna's life was a smorgasbord. People in her life constantly wanted "talents and helps" from her. Jenna needed to take the time to examine her strengths and gifts and choose her ministry based on the strengths God had given her and His guidance. Jenna addressed this problem, and she was healed.

At the other extreme, one of my dearest friends struggled for years because she was greatly gifted by God to minister in the church body, but her gifts were not appreciated in her local church. Her self-image was deeply wounded. She tried to stifle some of her precious gifts and use other of her gifts in the business world. She ended up filled with frustration, anxiety, and using antidepressants.

Some churches do not understand the place of women. They fail to study and apply Scripture's teachings about women. Christ has given women roles as His representatives within the church as well as without.

If you haven't been encouraged to get involved in your local church, talk humbly with the church leadership to see where you might be of most help. If there is no place for you to serve based on the strengths God has given you, you need to find a church that honors your involvement as Christ does. If you cannot serve in one church, you need to find one where you can.

Sometimes our ministries are well known in our local church and community and have a wide outreach. Sometimes our ministries are known only to us and our coworkers in the lunch room where we unofficially counsel. That decision is up to God.

In counseling women over many years, I've found the following principles to be key in identifying just exactly what ministries God has designed specifically for each one of us:

1. Write a list of the activities that give you the greatest satisfaction. Realize these leanings are from God. Next select your favorite three, listing first what you most enjoy doing.
2. Write a list of your positive qualities. Check the list with your

friends. This is not bragging but is an opportunity to give glory to God by finding further areas for service.

3. Decide whether you most enjoy working alone, with one partner, or on a team.

4. Look to see what God is already doing and where you might fit in.

5. Ask the Holy Spirit to direct you to needs not yet being met that match your gifts.

6. Consider your time commitments: Will your ministry interfere with your time with Christ or your family?

7. Once you have identified your ministry, perform it in a relaxed, balanced manner. Don't procrastinate, yet don't overdo.

8. Keep open the door to change. The strengths you use today may not be appropriate two years from now. Every six months to a year, reevaluate your strengths and interests.

9. There are many books and surveys available for identifying your spiritual gifts.* One of the greatest joys in the Christian life is identifying, applying, and developing the ministry gifts God has given each one of us.

10. Look for creative ways to use your strengths and interests in ministry in and out of church. "Let your light shine before men." Consider more than the typical ministries of music and teaching in the church. For example, Janie is gifted in organization. She helps the young adults in her fellowship group by going to their apartments or homes to help them organize their papers, their kitchens, their life. One young man raved about how his spiritual life had improved since Janie taught him to be more organized. He's now free of the drain of trying to manage a chaotic household and free to use his own gifts to better advantage. What a ministry he received!

Not every woman needs to take turns serving in the nursery or teaching Sunday school. I know it's hard to resist the pleas of the Sunday school superintendent, but by filling a job that you're not gifted or interested in, the task becomes less joyful, and you may even be depriving others of the opportunity to minister through their gifts.

🕮 *Exploring Scripture*

The admonition in Colossians 3:23–24 says, "Whatever you do, work at it with all your heart, as working for the Lord, not for men, since you know that you will receive an inheritance from the Lord as a reward. It is the Lord Christ you are serving" (NIV).

- How are we to minister and where do our rewards come from?

Galatians 1:10 says, "Am I now trying to win the approval of men, or of God? Or am I trying to please men? If I were still trying to please men, I would not be a servant of Christ" (NIV).

- Do we serve people or God?

 *Taking Action*

- What creative gift(s) do you have that you've never used for the Lord?

- How might you use these gifts in your life now?

Brainstorm with other women friends about how they see your gifts and interests. You might be surprised at what they say!

Dear Lord, I long to serve You with joy and with my whole heart. I long to hear Your voice telling me, "Well done." Help me to shut out the clamor of the demands of others and listen only to You. Help me to minister to my own family. Thank You for the assurance that when I minister as You have designed, I am pleasing You.

---

* My clients have found these books most helpful: *Unwrap Your Spiritual Gifts* by Kenneth Gangel (Victor, 1983); *Nineteen Gifts of the Spirit* by Leslie B. Flynn (Victor, 1994); and *Discovering Your Spiritual Gifts* by Kenneth Cain Kinghorn (Zondervan, 1984)—this last book is inexpensive and includes a personal inventory.

Controlling Your Image

*K*ristin's husband feels lucky to have married her. Kristin could be a model. She's a college graduate who worked as a stewardess before she married. But she hid a secret that tormented her until she finally got brave enough to discuss it with me in counseling— she believes everybody is smarter, prettier, and more capable than she is.

Kristin is one of a shocking number of beautiful, talented women who suffer from feelings of inferiority. Perhaps some slight as a child at a sensitive moment fueled feelings of rejection, and these beautiful women have not been satisfied with themselves since.

We all experience rejection at some stages of life. Rejection has many sources. We can be rejected because we have a strong positive quality that someone else envies. We can be rejected for our convictions or because of the people who are our associates. Perhaps we have been arrogant or unkind, and we really do need to learn better ways to relate to others. Perhaps we are unnecessarily sloppy or careless in our work or have followed bad habits of grooming and eating. Being rejected can take the form of a subtle snub or extreme rudeness. But if we are to enjoy healthy self-images, we must learn to deal with rejection because it will happen sometime.

Look at the apostle Paul. His rejection was such that people wanted to kill him! Acts 14:19–22 describes how some Jews turned the minds of the people against Paul, stoned him, and "dragged him out of the city thinking he was dead." How did Paul deal with it? Paul got up and walked back into the city! Did it bother Paul's self-image greatly? No. And the next day he was out preaching again, reminding the people that it is "through many tribulations that we must enter into the kingdom of God."

We may be poised, do everything "just right," have "perfect" bodies, gorgeous clothes, and wear costly perfumes and still feel inferior. What we really need is the beauty of holiness and the sweet fragrance of Christ.

God says over and over in His Word that we are precious. If we've never heard these words spoken with meaning by a parent or a spouse, we can hear God tell us whenever we set aside time to listen to Him. So let's act according to our worth to God—no matter how we may feel about it. He created us as we are and we are His. The choice is ours. God wants us to treasure ourselves no matter what our backgrounds may have done to us in the past or what our current physical or financial status may now be.*

 Exploring Scripture

Luke 12:15 says, ". . . a man's [or woman's] life does not consist in the abundance of his possessions" (NIV).

* What part do possessions play in projecting your image?

Taking Action

* Tell a close friend how you really feel about yourself. Ask the same friend what kind of image you project to others. Write her remarks here. Is that what you want to portray?

* List your good qualities others have said you have. Can you think of more?

❧

Lord, Thank You for making me just the way You did. Help me daily to concentrate on Your opinion of me and not all the negative thoughts I allow to fill my mind. Thank You for Your great love that You valued me enough to die for me. May I keep Your opinion of me uppermost in my mind all day long.

---

* Two books that will help you value yourself as God does are *Victory Over Darkness* by Neil T. Anderson (Regal Books, 1990) and *Search for Significance* by Robert McGee (Rapha Resources, 1990).

FIFTEEN

Giving Testimony

*S*traight from Webster's dictionary, testimony means "firsthand authentication of a fact." We can all give testimony about the facts of our daily lives. In a spiritual sense, however, what is our testimony? It's simply telling how God has reached each one of us. We tell our personal stories, and we testify that what God has done in our lives is true.

I'm going to share with you part of my own "testimony," my own story of how God has acted in my life. As you read it, think about how you came to know Jesus. What were your doubts and fears? How has He helped change you? What is your testimony?

When I was twenty-eight, if anybody asked me, I said I believed in a God who made me and made the world. Period. After originally making me, He was out of the picture. On my own I had achieved all my childhood dreams of marriage and motherhood. I expected to live like a fairy-tale princess—"happily ever after." Instead, however, I felt a vague emptiness. A sense of the meaninglessness of life brought confusion, and I sank into occasional depression.

I decided to go on my own hunt to find what, if anything, was of lasting value. I didn't realize that the emptiness of my life came from restlessness in my heart and that I longed for God.

I'd always been a churchgoer. I was brought up by my dad who took us to church regularly and by my mom who went to church on holidays. God was never mentioned outside of church or my parochial school. After my children were born, going to church seemed like too much trouble, so I started finding excuses to stay home.

Then I was talked into going on a retreat—a neighborhood women's getaway weekend. Some of the women had dramatic experiences with God there. I didn't. But after the retreat for the first time I began studying about the Christian religion. Prior to that I'd studied Eastern religions and practiced yoga, not seriously but simply from curiosity. After the retreat I read Scripture and stories about people relating to God as if He were right here instead of on a distant planet.

Shortly afterward, I became pregnant with my fourth child and had a medical crisis. I had to decide if I were willing to trust God with my life or not. I chose to believe that He did love me and had a plan for my life that was for my good and not for my harm.

I wanted to know more about His amazing power, so I studied and prayed. I asked Jesus to be my Lord and repented of my sins of the past. I said, "God, if there's more of You than I know and understand, show me; I open my life to You." My life, which had become dulled after the achievement of many of my life goals, took on a vibrant spiritual purpose and became more exciting and joyful than I'd ever known.

Prior to that I'd always believed in a "generic" God—not in a God who knows and cares about my every moment. After I came to believe in God's personal care, my husband, Wayne, came to believe as well.

Somehow I pray that God has touched you too. Will you tell others? We need to be willing to demonstrate love through our actions and words to every person we meet. Some people are amazed at the love they see us show and want to know why we care for them at all. We need to be ready to describe how God desires to relate to each person individually.

Scripture is filled with the testimony stories of Christ's followers. We can study these accounts for help in preparing our own testimonies. And we can pray about our encounters with others for Jesus. Being prepared to share our testimonies in bits and pieces with the clerk in the grocery story, the neighbor child who visits our home, or in a brief speech to anyone who wants to listen will not automatically lead others to Christ, but it may be an important step along someone's way. The more we practice the more we can avoid being impersonal, mechanical, rigid, or insensitive, and we can focus on being tender, kind, and persevering. (See 32, "Leading Others to Christ.")

Exploring Scripture

Second Peter 3:9 says, "The Lord is . . . not willing that any should perish but that all should come to repentance."

- Why should I give my testimony?

Second Timothy 4:2 reads, "Preach the word! Be ready in season and out of season. Convince, rebuke, exhort, with all longsuffering and teaching."

- How can I apply Paul's command in this verse?

Taking Action

- Based on your personal experiences with Christ, write your three-part testimony. Focus the first part briefly on your past, the second on how you came to know Jesus, and the last paragraph on what Christ has meant in your life.

Our testimonies need to be solidly based on Scripture. Three verses I recommend are

- Romans 3:23: "For all have sinned and fall short of the glory of God."
- First John 1: 9: "If we confess our sins, He [Jesus] is faithful and just to forgive us our sins and to cleanse us from all unrighteousness."
- John 1:12: "But as many as received Him, to them He gave the right to become children of God, to those who believe in His name."

Lord, I thank You for salvation in Jesus and for the joy You have given me. As I prepare my testimony, may I only include what is most pleasing to You and helpful to others.

Keeping Body and Soul Fit

We are part of a body-conscious generation. Women—who used to make fun of high school gym classes—now flock to health clubs and aerobics classes. After exercising, women can gain energy, feel better, and look better! Women who don't exercise often harbor tinges of guilt—even as they tease their friends who do!

As I counsel clients, two of the important areas I consider are the client's physical health *and* the client's spiritual health. Many women neglect both their bodies and their souls resulting in depression, irritability with spouses, and feelings of inadequacy. Our bodies and our souls atrophy from lack of exercise.

Fitness requires spiritual, mental, and physical knowledge and effort. In order to keep weariness from seeping into our bodies and souls, we need to set both physical-fitness goals for our bodies and spiritual-fitness goals for our souls. Then we need to work consistently toward achieving them.

Our body and soul goals are appropriate as long as they challenge us and they're attainable and measurable. Physically our goals might be walking a mile or running a marathon. Spiritually our goals might be daily prayer, reading three chapters of Scripture daily, getting through the Bible in a year, or memorizing one verse each week.

Along with setting these goals, it often surprises clients when I discuss nutrition. Nutritional goals correlate with physical and spiritual fitness goals and are important aids in achieving these goals. We need to eat from all four food groups each day, use stimulants only in moderation or avoid them altogether, and maintain proper amounts of vitamins and minerals in our diets.

I counseled a young man in his late twenties who was suicidal. He couldn't understand why breakfast of sugared cereal, no lunch, and dinner at McDonald's five times a week was inadequate nutrition and would affect his appreciation of life. By improving his diet along with healing his emotional hurts through our counseling sessions, he was able to change his "victim" thought patterns and restore his enthusiasm for life.

I am continually amazed at how many of my clients do not eat healthy, well-balanced meals. The hardest part is convincing clients that an adequate physical and spiritual diet is worth trying; it seems too easy. I explain to clients that they may not need to see me as long for counseling if they correct their nutrition—physically and spiritually. I suggest trying dietary changes while they receive counseling. Afterward, the benefits become obvious to them.

We can check our spiritual diets in the same way we check our physical diets. We're bombarded with suggestions to limit sugar and fat, increase raw fiber and fresh fruits, and eat food as natural to the source as possible. That's exactly how our study of God's Word should be—as direct and fresh as possible! As food moves through the refining processes, some nutrients are lost, and the personal meaning of God's Word is sometimes lost as well when it's processed through others.

We eat meals three times a day. Are we willing to eat three spiritual meals a day too?

Here's a suggested menu:

Breakfast: By using a written prayer, we can praise God for His holiness, faithfulness, and love and bring before Him the particular needs of the day.

Lunch: Reading an article or part of a book or listening to a teaching tape is a great way to enjoy a spiritual lunch. Tucking a small book into our purses and pulling it out at break or at lunch or putting on a tape at home—the children will enjoy it too—are easy ways to enjoy lunch.

Dinner: Another time for soul food is mealtime prayer with the family.

Bedtime: We can't forget a bedtime snack! We'll sleep so much better! Just as sleep experts often recommend a snack like a bowl of cereal or a piece of toast before bed, spiritual food helps us sleep, too. We can ask God for one new truth before we end the day. We need a steady diet of God the Father, Son, and Spirit all day long.

After our spiritual and physical diet comes fitness activities. Notice I don't say exercise. Who wants to exercise? It sounds like work. But if we say walk, play tennis, stretch, or play, it seems more inviting, and we're more eager to find something we like to do and get out and do it! That's the key.

We can ask other people to join us to make our exercise a social time or maybe a chance to minister to others. Young children might enjoy biking with us; a neighbor we otherwise wouldn't have time to visit might enjoy walking with us.

Maybe it seems selfish to waste time on ourselves. Wrong! Our bodies are the *temples* of the Holy Spirit. Consider the care the temple of Jerusalem required for upkeep. Are we less valuable? (See 7, "Decorating Our Temples.") The Lord is honored if we're a healthy weight, take care of our skin, and have a decent haircut regularly.

And, of course, we need rest. How do we get spiritual rest? Nature is a strong reflection of God. (See 12, "Playing Like a Child" and 29, "Refreshing Yourself.")

Prayer helps us choose any new activity. Making changes in our lifestyles when we're sure they're what God wants helps us avoid changes that come from the pressure of others. We need to recognize the physical and spiritual benefits for ourselves. Then we have the *desire* to make the changes.

Exploring Scripture

Third John 2 reads, "Beloved, I pray that you may prosper in all things and be in health, just as your soul prospers."

- How does this verse illustrate the connection between the body and the soul?

Taking Action

- What are your physical fitness goals?

- List three steps you will take to reach your goals:

- What are your spiritual fitness goals?

- List three steps you will take to reach your goals:

Lord, my body, mind, and spirit belong to You. Help me to care for them all wisely—feeding, exercising, and resting them as a precious temple.

Chasing Shadows

The shadow of worry can settle over any person's life. Chasing shadows is what we do when we worry. Despite the prevalence of worry, I seldom have someone come into my office for counseling to get free of worry. Instead, clients want to remove every situation from their lives that they worry over. That's impossible.

Where does a tendency to worry come from? Ultimately from sin—the same sin Eve dealt with—a desire to be in control, to know everything, to be like God. Then it filters through our heredity and our environment.

Nancy revealed in counseling that her mom had a tendency to always say, "I'm worried. I'm worried that my car won't start . . . that you'll be too cold in that coat . . . that . . ." Nancy picked up her "worry language" subconsciously from her mom.

Even more than the words themselves, Nancy picked up worry as a habitual way of responding. While some personality types—the more sensitive, deep thinkers who see the "what-ifs" around every corner—have a stronger temptation toward worry, outgoing, carefree personality types like Nancy have learned to worry by seeing parents use worry as a way of responding to situations. When Nancy worried, she undermined her ability to realistically evaluate problems.

I've observed a curious thing about worry in the women I've counseled. Many of these women face the bigger issues of life such as a husband's illness or the loss of a home with greater inner peace and calm than they face minor problems. I've concluded this variation exists because God gives grace to deal with the *real* trials of life, both large and small, so that worry isn't necessary. People who worry continually are not experiencing God's grace in the smaller matters of life.

Nancy was tied up with worry over trivial details. She knew she was driving her husband crazy, and he insisted she get help. She said she came to see me about marriage problems. In one session it was obvious worry had crept over every aspect of Nancy's life. It dimmed her joy, her confidence, and her peace.

After studying the biblical principles related to worry, Nancy was surprised to learn that worry is a sin and a temptation to worry must be resisted. I explained that worry is every bit as bad as overeating or self-centeredness and that worry damaged her relationship with God. You can't trust God totally and worry at the same time!

I encouraged Nancy to let tomorrow worry about itself, but tomorrow can't worry because it's not a person. Isn't that exactly why Jesus used the example? That means there's to be no worrying. Mother Teresa faces death from disease every day of her life and has for decades, yet she joyfully prays and goes about her business without a trace of worry.

Worry creates fear, and it's difficult to think and plan clearly when we have fear. That sneaky old Devil wants us to become locked in fear so we'll flop in our physical and spiritual and emotional life. As God's children, we need to tell him to get lost.

God tells us not to live in fear. Some women hear accounts of husbands running off with their secretaries and they think, "That could be me. Can I really rely on his love?" Yes and no. We can always rely on God's love. We can't get a guarantee from our husbands. All we can do is pray for our husbands' protection. If he's not a Christian, we can pray daily for his conversion and ask God to safeguard him in the meantime. We can concentrate on being the kind of loving, sweet, affectionate wife no man in his right man would want to leave. And we must forget our fears!

Think of worry as a dirty word! It is a temptation that God knew we'd have. God made it perfectly clear how we are to deal with it—DON'T WORRY!! Refusing to worry is often an act of the will.

Look at Jesus, our supreme example. Jesus was fully human. Did He worry? No! He faced the future realistically, but not with worry. Jesus shed tears for us because we would reject His work of the Cross. There's no denying He said, "Let this cup pass." The night of His betrayal was an incredibly painful part of His sacrifice. Jesus was rejected by those He loved. But He didn't spend His life prior to the Last Supper and the Crucifixion saying, "I'm so worried." He said in effect, "Hey guys, My betrayal and death are going to happen, so don't worry or be surprised." Jesus knew why He came. We know why we're here, too, to glorify God by our trust, to witness for Him, and to die. So why dread anything in life? After this life comes the "happiness forever" part.

Exploring Scripture

Matthew 6:25–28 is the famous worry passage. "Therefore I tell you, do not worry about your life, what you will eat or drink; or about your body, what you will wear. Is not life more important than food, and the body more important than clothes? Look at the birds of the air; they do not sow or reap or store away in barns, and yet your heavenly Father feeds them. Are you not much more valuable than they? Who of you by worrying can add a single hour to his life?" (NIV). Take time to study this passage in several different Bible translations to get the full impact of its meaning.

Notice Jesus taught the "Our Father" (Matthew 6:9–13) right alongside this passage. We're told not to worry and we're told what to do—pray and ask the Father to give us our daily bread, to protect us from evil. As we remind ourselves of His holiness and power (hallowed be Your name), we ask that only His will be done and we remind ourselves that His kingdom is coming. And as we forgive and ask forgiveness, there's no worry that we're not in a right relationship with God the Father, Son, and Spirit. What a perfect antidote to worry! Trust in the Father!

Taking Action

- What kind of things do you typically worry over? List them here.

- Will you commit yourself to be accountable to share with a friend your efforts to stop worrying? Write her name here.

Philippians 4:6 says, "Don't worry over anything whatever; tell God every detail of your needs in earnest and thankful prayer, and the peace of God which transcends human understanding, will keep constant guard over your hearts and minds as they rest in Christ Jesus" (PHILLIPS).

- What are we to do when the urge to worry comes?

- Look up Philippians 4:4–6 in your Bible and write out the entire section using your name in place of the pronouns.

We take a powerful preventive measure when we allow God to help us not worry today. This is the kind of help the Holy Spirit gives us. Jesus told the apostles not to worry even about what they were to say if they were arrested. He said the Holy Spirit would tell them what to say. Whatever the situation, rely on the Holy Spirit instead of worrying.

Lord, my long list of worries does not come from You, for You give Your grace for each day. Thank You that You've told me over and over again that You love me and You are caring for me. Thank You that every day and every aspect of my life is in Your hands.

Preventing Family Problems

*U*sing biological terms, psychologists have described the family as a system made up of organs (family members). The system works best when all the organs are healthy and working together according to the same guidelines.

What are some of the guidelines that keep family systems running well? Here are some counseling strategies we can learn that will help us have smoother relationships with the members of our families. As you read through each item, ask God to show you if it applies to you.

- If you don't expect any member of the family to think or act as you would, you won't be disappointed.

   You can point out the advantages of a desirable action, but if the other person is an adult, you need to let go of your desires for him or her. If your children are still "under your roof," you have more control, but they still have a free will. Modeling the behavior and values you'd like your children to develop is the best teacher.

- Communicate clearly your feelings and needs to your husband and children and encourage them to do likewise.

   A client of mine in her late sixties never told her children when she needed their help with a chore or when she missed them. She expected her children to anticipate her needs. Her frequent phrases were "They should know" and "If I have to tell them to help me, I'd as soon they not do it."

   "Why?" I asked her. "With the busy lifestyle of your grown children, what's wrong with being direct with the people close to you?"

- Be wary of providing "overcare" for family members.

   That means avoid repeatedly doing things for others they can do themselves. Overcare can damage your relationships with the people you're helping who may then begin to feel guilty. As long as you allow yourself to be used, you're tempting someone to use you. This is true of your children as well as your husband or extended family.

- Listen carefully to the feelings family members express.

  Use common sense to evaluate their needs and decide how to respond—children who balk at going to bed don't benefit from staying up late, but as long as they can get away with it, they will.

- Make sure your self-image include outlets besides taking care of others.

  Jesus says that you are significant to God, but not because of your works. Build an image of yourself that depends on what Jesus said and did for you and not on what you say and do.

- Avoid triangular conversation.

  If you tell your feelings to a son or daughter and want the child to communicate them back to your husband, an unfair burden is placed on the child who gets stuck in the middle. A child who doesn't want to relay a message risks feeling guilty and fears your anger. If they do express it, they're worried their other parent will be angry or hurt.

- Take time to get emotional and physical rest.

  Be sure to consider your personal needs or you won't be able to relate healthily to anybody else. Otherwise you can easily become resentful as you meet others' needs and try to make those you love happy.

- Every family has its own set of rules.

  Some of your familial rules may have come from your own childhoods. You brought them into your family without even consciously thinking about it. These rules affect how you show your joy, your anger, how you deal with stress or conflict, how you act toward others. Family rules are typically not spoken in words directly, but everybody hears them very clearly just the same. You need to examine them occasionally to see which, if any, you need to change.

Here are some examples of *unhealthy* family rules:

- Be a high achiever and make sure what you're doing is always productive.
- Work harder and work longer hours than necessary to get ahead.
- Deny your own feelings when someone else in the family is upset. (How can you think about yourself at a time like this?)
- Children, even when grown, are second-class citizens. (Have you ever witnessed a successful businessman who acts the part of mommy's little boy when he goes home? He's never allowed to be an adult around his parents.)
- Talk only about what's pleasant. When someone makes a mistake, don't discuss it. Converse about abstract subjects like sports, world events, and jobs rather than personal issues.
- Only talk about troubles and problems. When one member has a problem or disappointment, discuss it over and over and beat the topic to death.
- Be two different people. (Swing between demanding to be pleased right now, and "I don't care what you do" later.)

The family needs to be our one safe place where each one of us as family members can admit weaknesses and not be laughed at or criticized—where family members are always pulling for us not against us. We can alter any family rules that we no longer feel are right. The Bible is the guidebook for the kind of rules our family systems should have, not the voices and rules of the past. All of our families can benefit from examining our systems in the light of Scripture regularly.

Some families would rather live in constant tension than risk change. That can lead to denial of problems and keep everyone walking on eggshells, often resulting in physical symptoms such as headaches, insomnia, and stomach pain that go along with family problems. We need to risk "being emotionally intimate" with our families. It's never healthy to isolate ourselves.

📖 *Exploring Scripture*

Read Ephesians 3:14–15: "For this reason I bow my knees to the Father of our Lord Jesus Christ, from whom the whole family in heaven and earth is named."

Where does the concept of family come from? The concept of family comes from God and belongs first to Him because we are part of His divine family. God ordained that a man and woman come together in marriage and become an indissoluble union.

✑ Taking Action

- Write down any unhealthy family rules that you need to change.

Are you presently dealing with a family problem? Try handling it God's way:

1. Discuss it in love.
2. Do not be judgmental or critical.
3. Listen to and repeat aloud how the other person is feeling to make sure you understand correctly.
4. Brainstorm ways to solve the problem. Look for a solution both sides find agreeable.
5. Be willing to compromise out of love on any issue that is not contrary to God's law or His Word.

❦

Dear Lord, sometimes the voices of the past govern how I treat those I love today. Clear my mind and heart of the destructive voices of the past, and help me to follow Your ways in keeping the relationships and communications healthy in my family.

✎ NINETEEN ✎

Giving Generously

*G*enerosity is a quality we best teach our children by practicing it. A friend of mine occasionally pays the highway tolls for herself *and* the car behind her when she goes through the toll booth. She calls this a RAOK, a Random Act Of Kindness. Do you suppose her children sitting in the back seat are getting the idea? How wonderful it would be if we all sprinkled our worlds with random acts of kindness! Even millionaires who give generously to others are blessed when they are treated generously by someone else.

Although most of us as Christian women admit that God needs to get the first fruits, the tithe, a tenth of everything that comes in the house, as soon as things get financially tough, it can be tempting to cut that out. But giving to others is essential in our Christian lives! It's a law as true as gravity—if we give, we will receive. What goes up, comes down. We can't explain how it works, it just does. GIVE!! If our husbands refuse to give, we can pray for God to change their minds and, in the meantime, look for other ways in which we can practice generosity.

In America we're about to lose the last of the generation who lived through the depression and World War II. During the depression, a company sometimes bought a truckload of potatoes and sold them at a fraction of the cost to their employees or provided coal during the winter for those laid off.

When there were few true jobs, people with money found odd jobs around their houses that those in need could do. Those jobs included paying neighbor women to bake bread for them rather than buying it from local markets or hiring men for garden work and cleanup. During the depression, government welfare provided food but not money. People looked out for one another with generosity and kindness. It was a unique time in our history.

Today, in order to have extra finances to give to others, it helps to develop the quality of thriftiness. A thrifty person is not a hoarder or cheap and stingy but rather is a person who has a healthy perspective toward material possessions. More and more women are realizing every day that less can be better and inexpensive is fine as long as the quality is adequate. Recently I attended a lecture by a fashion consultant wearing a stylish outfit. She confided to the audience that she'd purchased everything, including her shoes, at secondhand stores.

We don't need lots of clothes, and we don't necessarily need expensive ones, but we should be neatly dressed with a sense of confidence—remember we're representatives of Christ! When we shop, do we buy only sale items? Thrift is fine when our purposes is to have extra to share with others, but does that mean God's people need to be cheap? God can afford to pay full price sometimes. There's a fine line between being a careful spender and being obsessive about bargains.

Whenever an unexpected expense comes up, try saying, "Well Lord, instead of being discouraged by this, I'm going to see how I can give an extra gift to You."

Give generously of time and effort. Teach your children when you go to a public park or restroom to always leave the place a little better than they found it, to think about the next person who will be using it. Practice thinking of ways to be generous to others!

How simple can it be to have a generous attitude? Work hard, save carefully, spend wisely, and give generously.

Exploring Scripture

Proverbs 11:25 tells us, "The generous soul will be made rich, and he who waters will also be watered himself."

- In what ways can we become rich that don't involve money?

In 2 Corinthians 8:9 we read, "For you know the grace of our Lord Jesus Christ, that though he was rich, yet for your sakes he became poor, so that you through his poverty might become rich" (NIV).

- How is this an example of God's grace?

- How should God's grace motivate us to be generous people?

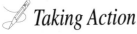 *Taking Action*

- If looking out for the welfare of others in your community was solely your responsibility, how would you go about it?

- What can you do to practice and teach more generosity in your home?

Lord, there is a difference between thriftiness and being cheap, between generosity and being a spendthrift. Help me to know the difference—and to be both generous and wise.

Forgiving Others

The two greatest commandments are "Love the LORD, your God, with all your heart, soul, and mind, and love your neighbor as yourself."

Those are the commandments that my client Leah had to apply, but she didn't take Scripture seriously, or she would never had to come to see me. Most of us have often dealt with anger and minor irritations. Leah had too, but when she came to see me, she was struggling with a feeling brand new to her as a Christian. Someone in her family had hurt her deeply, and that person refused to admit the wrong. Leah became livid with rage whenever she thought of it, which was often, and the rage didn't go away over several months. Leah finally sought professional counseling.

Her exact words in describing her situation were, "Now I understand how someone can become so angry with another person that they want to kill."

I said, "Leah, Jesus stressed the importance of forgiving because He knew Satan would use dissension to destroy people."

Without blinking she answered, "I know, but I can't."

Can't? Leah was a mature Christian with forty years of walking with God, but she'd been deeply hurt.

I asked Leah if she could pray for the person who had wronged her. Leah looked as if I'd asked her to stick a knife in herself. She said that was impossible. She didn't know how she'd ever be able to pray for that person's good. I suggested she pray simply that God would deal with the individual with justice and mercy. Leah considered that several seconds and then agreed she could try that.

Forgiveness is a basic principle of the Christian life, but somehow it looks easier to practice when it's written in a book than it does when it hits the area of a painful relationship in our own lives. Praying for our enemies is the Christian weapon God has given us to fight the temptations of Satan to hate our enemies and be filled with bitterness. Praying softens our hearts so that we can forgive.

I've seen Christian testimonies destroyed over and over again because a person wouldn't take the step of praying for an enemy. An enemy is anyone who has done a wrong to us, whether it's a real wrong or just perceived by us as a wrong. Either way our prayers involve God in the solution of restoring love in our hearts.

This is "square one" in the Christian life. It's so basic. Everyone *knows* this, but we need to apply it in situations where it seems impossible. That's what surrendering to the lordship of Christ over every area of our lives means.

Won't people think we're weak and wimpy and we're letting people walk all over us? So what? To forgive shows greater strength and composure than reacting harshly to someone else's personal attacks. God wants us to live in harmony, shouldn't we want the same? Even if we don't want to, we must. To show how important forgiveness is, Jesus said, "But if you do not forgive men their trespasses, *neither will your Father forgive your trespasses*" (Matthew 6:15, italics mine). Furthermore, forgiveness needs to come *from our hearts* (see Matthew 18:21–35, especially v. 35).

When Carla's husband told her he didn't want to be married to her anymore, he said, "You can have the profit from the house." She said, "I'll be investing my share in another house, but I want you to know that I still consider this partly your money. And when I do sell, you'll benefit too."

That's the love that makes people stop and think, "What is it about these Christians?" "See how they love." "Why aren't they looking out for themselves?" "Do they truly have a heavenly Father who watches out for them?" (It's a lot easier to be fearless, loving, and forgiving when you know that.) Is it tough? You bet! By the grace of God it can be done. Romans 8:28 says, "All things work together for good to those who love God, to those who are called according to His purpose."

Exploring Scripture

Read John 8:1–11 where real guilt encounters God's grace.

- Who are the "guilty" parties in this incident?

- Who's perfect? I'm not. "Little" sins, "big" sins—they're all the same to God. Through the process of forgiveness, He gives us freedom to fix things up when we fail or somebody fails us. Couldn't Jesus say to each of us what He told the people who brought the adulterous woman to Him? "He who is without sin among you, let him throw a stone at her first" (John 8:7).

Taking Action

- Who has wronged you in the past or maybe is still offending you right now?

- Write a brief sentence promising to forgive the person(s) and pray for their welfare.

- Prayer is "Part I." "Part II" is "do good to those who hurt you." That's even tougher, but so powerful. What good can you *do* for the person(s) listed above who has offended you?

Lord, it's so hard to forgive when I feel so used and deceived.
Only Your grace and power flowing through me as I
continually bring this person before You in prayer will ever
bring forgiveness into my heart. Thank You for Your mercy,
and fill me with a loving heart and a
willingness to be kind.

TWENTY–ONE

Imitating Great Women

"Mentoring" is a popular concept today. The Bible, timeless in its message, speaks of mentoring in Titus 2:4, "That they [the older women] may teach the young women to be sober, to love their husbands, to love their children, to be discreet, chaste, keepers at home, good, obedient to their own husbands, that the word of God be not blasphemed" (KJV).

Mentoring is the process of learning from a wise and trusted teacher. It can occur by imitating the behavior of a person alive now or a historical figure like a woman from the pages of Scripture.

Let's look at the "number one" model of womanhood in the Bible—Mary, the mother of Jesus. How highly God thought of this woman to choose her for His divine conception! What qualities can we learn from her life?

Go back in time and imagine the anguish and confusion of Mary as she stood at the cross and heard her Son Jesus say, "It is finished." Then He dropped His head and died as she stood watching in agony.

Imagine Mary thinking, "Gabriel, you didn't mention this part. This was not the end I expected." Mary, above all others, knew the power her Son possessed. She probably saw private miracles before the wedding at Cana, or she wouldn't have asked Jesus to perform a wine-making miracle.

Consequently, Mary knew Jesus had power over the cross. Yet she watched Him choose to endure it. And the Father allowed Mary's Son to die in her presence. But the angel Gabriel had said Jesus would occupy the throne of David. Mary also would have expected an earthly king. How could Mary make sense of that? She had to wonder.

How did Mary respond? In steadfast obedience. Mary continued to do the things expected of her. We read about her going to pray with the apostles after Jesus' death. Acts 1:14 says, "They all joined together constantly in prayer, along with the women and Mary the mother of Jesus, and with his brothers" (NIV). She continued to trust God and pray. Wouldn't we have loved to witness her joy when she saw Jesus alive again?!

A client of mine, the wife of a prominent local businessman, lost two sons four years apart, but she never lost her belief in a loving, powerful God. I will love seeing her joyful reunion with her sons in heaven some day! In the meantime this woman goes right on keeping on. Is this a message to those around her? You bet.

We may know that God has the power to change difficult situations we're going through right now, but we wait and wait for a change, and He doesn't do it. Can we keep on keeping on? What kind of model of womanhood are we providing for our children and our children's children?

Exploring Scripture

Look at some other great women who are described in Scripture, and you'll see more qualities worth imitating. Esther 4:1—When challenge came into Esther's life, she was ready. Luke 8:2—Mary Magdalene's life teaches that nothing in our past can prevent us from loving and serving Christ. Judges 4:4–5—Deborah was a talented woman who demonstrated creativity and leadership abilities. Ruth 1:1–4:22—Ruth was persistent and steadfast.

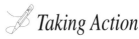 Taking Action

- If your life were written up as a Bible story, what would it say about your faith? Write a brief paragraph.

Lord, I need to be mentored by Christlike women and I need to be a mentor for others. Give me eyes to see the best *examples in those around me, and help me to never forget that others are watching me.*

❧ TWENTY–TWO ❧

Sanctifying Your Home

I dreamed one night of young children asleep in their beds. The headboards of their beds were molded plastic half-wheels with wide spokes. Each child's name was at the center of their half-wheel. Scripture verses, which uniquely applied to each child's life, were hand-printed on each spoke.

This dream signified to me the order God gave all parents in Deuteronomy 6. Each one of us has been given the command to diligently teach God's Word to our children, the neighborhood children, and our grandchildren. The Jews use a mezuzah (a scroll containing these verses) attached on their doorposts which they touch every time they enter to remind them of God's Word in verse 9: "You shall write [His commands] on the doorposts of your house and on your gates."

Why should we sanctify our homes? Because we want to make our homes places where others can experience God. How do we make our homes holy? Here are some ideas that may help.

When we moved from one home to another, we had a house dedication ceremony with our friends. My husband and I, our children, our pastor, and our Christian friends walked through our home, stopping frequently to pray and dedicate it to God. If you haven't already asked God's blessing upon your home, I strongly urge you to do so.

As a reminder, at the garage door entrance and on the deck, somewhere prominent, we've posted the words contained in Joshua 24:15, "As for me and my house, we will serve the LORD." When our daughters married, we purchased housewarming gifts of God's Word written on refrigerator magnets and wall hangings.

The music, the pictures, the books of our homes can advertise Christ to our children and our guests. I recently visited the National Gallery of Art in London, England, and was reminded again that the majority of great art has had a Christian theme for centuries. Certainly not every picture in our homes has to have a specifically Christian theme, but certainly several should.

Kathy has decorated her living room and kitchen along the theme of the vine and the branches (John 15:5–8). She has ivy wallpaper, and a local artist painted ivy on one of her walls. Her other decorations tie the theme together exquisitely. Whenever anyone comments, Kathy explains the story of the vine and the branches and her position of clinging to Christ.

In Deuteronomy 6:6 God commands talking about the Word at meals, discussing Bible principles at bedtime and throughout the day, and making our homes places where others can grow closer to God. We can keep a box of Bible verses on the kitchen table and have each child pick a verse (read it for the little ones) and talk about how it applies to their day.

Each of us can discover what triggers a reminder of God's love and presence in our homes and in the minds and hearts of ourselves and our children. These are not meant to be just the cultural trappings of Christianity but springboards for thought and prayer. It's easy to forget without reminders to help.

In our daily conversations we can help our children appreciate God's signs in the world around them. We must never be indifferent to the hand of God in things like sunsets, cloud formations, and storms. We can enjoy the beauty of people and point out their fascinating features to our children.

Exploring Scripture

John 14:23 says, "Jesus answered and said to him, 'If anyone loves Me, he will keep My word; and My Father will love him, and We will come to him and make Our home with him.'"

- What is the source of your home's holiness?

- Psalm 127 is the Scripture we used for our home dedication. What does it say about our work and about family?

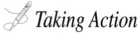 *Taking Action*

- Make a list of the steps you will take to dedicate your home to the Lord.

- What additional meaningful symbols or actions can you use in your home to remind you that your body, your home, your life is sanctified for God?

ᴄᴏ᙭ᴏ

Lord, be present in our home, filling it with Your love and wisdom. I want to decorate our home with those pictures and ornaments that daily increase our knowledge and awareness of You, and may I never forget that our home is dedicated to You.

TWENTY THREE

Keeping the Joy

*A*rlene, a thirty-year-old mom, came to see me because she'd lost her zest for life. I've often seen this listlessness in moms who feel trapped by child care and work. I've also seen it in older women with grown children who thought they'd be happy in those later quiet years of their lives and instead have become irritable and depressed, and I've seen this listlessness in single women who long for a husband and a family.

Whatever our age or circumstances, here are some tips to keep the joy in our lives at any age.

- We can choose to refuse to lose our joy.

  Irritations can steal our emotional joy. Every day some things will happen that can get us in a dither. Sometimes we can correct them, but more often we must simply commit ourselves to keep our joyful spirit despite our circumstances.

- We can hunt for joy and seek beauty and harmony no matter what.

  We can keep our inner selves cheerful and pleasant by finding something to enjoy in every moment—the beauty in the way the rays of the sun illuminate a room, a cloud formation, someone's smile, the colors of fresh vegetables in a salad, or even the smell of a fragrant cleaning product!

  Our son David was diagnosed with cancer, and four months later, while out jogging, he was hit by a drunk driver. The accident shattered his leg and put him in a thigh-high cast. He and I spent 160 days in the hospital in one year. Every day we found something to smile, chuckle, and sometimes even laugh about. We chose to refuse to lose our joy.

- We can sprinkle our lives regularly with new experiences.

  A new experience can be a book we read, a day as a volunteer, a change in our recreation, a day's outing, or a new blouse. A long vacation qualifies too, but the new experience doesn't have to be elaborate. It always helps to have some event that we're planning for the future. The planning is as therapeutic as the experience. The side benefit is that we have interesting plans to discuss and stories to share with the people around us. We don't need to settle for a humdrum life. We can choose to refuse to lose our joy.

- We can live each moment without regret.

That's what Jesus meant when He said to find joy again and again all the time in Him, in His Creation, in His plan for our lives. "Rejoice in the Lord always." Our future fun will turn out to be only as good as our present fun because the present becomes the future tomorrow. The past is never to be again. Everyone's past is full of pain, mistakes, injustices—those we caused and those done to us. We can't mentally beat ourselves up over the past. Also, if we have a physical limitation, we can't dwell on it; everyone has something. We *can* stop thinking about it and talking about it. Chances are the people close to us have heard enough. We can get on with doing fully what we can do right now. We can choose to refuse to lose our joy.

- When we need to make a decision, we can pray first and then follow our natural inclinations and not stew over decisions.

Many young women I've counseled have been tied in knots because of indecision about the future. Of all the decisions to be made, most are minor, after all. Don't stew and huff and puff over every little thing. I used to spend five minutes studying the menu in a restaurant and then usually order something I didn't like as much as the entree served to someone else at my table. Now I skim the menu and make a decision. I'd rather enjoy the company of the people I'm with or the book I brought to read if I'm alone. Decision-making over insignificant as well as important things can require far too much time. Some of our choices will be "wrong," but most are not really worth groaning over. Far better to get on with finding the good in the choices we have made. We can choose to refuse to lose our joy.

- We can find a measure of satisfaction in the work we must do now.

We can learn to do it well, whether it's working on the assembly line or designing fashions. Each day we are alive we can be aware of our senses as we work; we can feel the pen or the computer keys, the texture of the bags we fill, or the arm we stick an IV needle into. We can take time to smile at a baby and be pleased with the wiggles and stretches when we try to change a diaper. We can be happy that our health allows us to be productive. Finding pleasure in work is therapeutic. Just because we *must* do something doesn't mean we wouldn't choose to do it, even if we didn't have to. We can balance our work with an activity we'd love to do even without pay, like creating something or collecting something for a hobby. We can choose to refuse to lose our joy.

- We can decide to be satisfied with who we are, with what we're able to do physically and afford financially; we can make a habit of satisfaction and not dreary resignation.

   Even if we can afford a nice speed boat, it's still fun to experience the pleasure of a rowboat or a canoe occasionally. Even if we can afford to eat out at gourmet restaurants every night, we can try a picnic in the park now and then and explore the library and museums for music and art and stimulating ideas; we can take up an inexpensive hobby. Finding free and inexpensive sources of joy keep us free from dependence on money for our pleasure. We can choose to refuse to lose our joy.

Exploring Scripture

Jesus didn't sit in one place. He was often on the go, traveling to new places, meeting different people. Get involved and stay active.

How did Jesus feel about joy? Look up the great attitude sections in the Bible as recorded in Matthew 5:1–12 and Luke 6:20–23.

In effect, these verses say: When you don't have enough money, you're hungry or sad, or people are against you and reject you, when things aren't going well, "Rejoice *in that day* and leap for joy [When? Then, in that day, when it's happening! Why?], for indeed your reward is great in heaven" (Luke 6:23). And in so doing you *choose to refuse to lose your joy.*

Taking Action

- Have you lost your joy in any of the seven areas described? Record what steps you will take now to make the necessary changes in your attitude and lifestyle in order to choose to keep your joy.

- Write down other ways you can teach your children to live joyfully, no matter what.*

Lord, living a joyful life is a decision that I must make. Help me daily to choose to see the opportunities for joy all around me and to refuse to lose the joy that comes from You.

---

* Read *The Christian's Secret of a Happy Life* by Hannah Whitall Smith. Written in the late 1800s, this book is incredibly relevant today because of its strong and practical scriptural foundation.

Releasing Creativity

We are creative people because we're made in the image and likeness of God, the Creator of all things. God created, and then He stood back and admired. Maybe the results of our creative efforts are less than we'd planned, still we've made something that wasn't before. That alone is fulfilling.

Unless we look for opportunities to be creative, we'll mainly be consumers of the creativity of others. Unfortunately, that's not emotionally satisfying enough for children or adults because we have an inner need to use our talents. Being creative is psychotherapeutic; not creating is a deprivation. How then can we release the creativity within us?

Cooking, collecting, journaling, crafting, gourmet cooking, home decorating, paper-folding, painting, writing letters or poetry are all proven creative outlets. We can try them all to see what we love doing the most.

Ever wonder why food has to be prepared? Couldn't God have given us food that didn't have to be peeled, trimmed, chopped, sliced, and sometimes cooked? Sure! But quite possibly He knew we'd need the creative satisfaction that preparation allows. Combine, spread, smush. Cooking can be very creative, and its a fun way to teach creativity to our children also. Although many of the past avenues for creativity such as cooking, sewing, and weaving are no longer essential, they're still worth doing for fun.

Creativity doesn't have to be costly. Deciding how to make do with what we have can be a creative activity—like cutting off long pants to make shorts when summer comes.

When we gather for a family party, we have five children under seven years of age. Instead of having the adults visit together while the children play, we try to have at least one activity where adults and children interact.

The last weekend in October our family celebrated fall. It was too cold to play an outdoor game like badminton or croquet, so we went on a leaf hunt. My sister, Joy, and I gave her son and each of my grandchildren a bag and went for a walk in the woods to find ten gorgeous leaves. Then we returned to the house and gathered around the table. Each child had an adult to help, and we passed out fingerpaint paper and gobs of paint. After smearing around some background colors, each child stuck the leaves decoratively on the paper. The results were not Michelangelo, but the children will remember our activity because it was creative and we did it together. What a great chance to enjoy God's beauty and grow closer to another adult member of the family.

Creative fun takes a tiny bit of thinking ahead. Preschool activity or school art books can provide ideas.

If our children see us enjoying a creative activity, they'll be more likely to want to participate on their own. When my children were little, I was a full-time homemaker and I sewed most of their clothes. My daughters wanted to sit with me and make doll clothes and eventually their own clothes.

Collecting can be a creative enterprise. I've seen beautiful collections of salt and pepper shakers or glass bottles. Some people decorate with a theme of an animal or a fruit and collect roosters or cows or strawberries. Everyone can get involved in the fun of buying items to add to their collections, and they don't have to be expensive original art.

Some women find time to play an instrument; others write music. Having a creative hobby they love enhances rather than detracts from their child-rearing and homemaking roles.

Keep a journal not only for the therapeutic value of recording feelings but also for the creative task of putting words on paper. How many Louisa May Alcotts are out there?

My husband, Wayne, wrote a poem when we visited the lakes area of England, and I read the poem to our grandsons. Now six-year-old Jack carries a notebook around with him and writes his own poems. Had we never introduced this to Jack, would he ever have gotten excited about writing poetry? I doubt it. We have fun hearing Jack read his poems to us over the phone. His mom helps him write them down, of course.

My mother taught me to be creative. In grade school I wanted to dress like everyone else, wear the same colors and even the same coat at times. She'd say over and over, "Be different, be yourself; you don't have to look, act, and think the same." And my father taught me to try different jobs and activities. He communicated that he was sure I could always do anything. My parents passed a willingness to be creative on to me, and that's what I want to give to my family. What attitudes towards creativity do you want to pass on?

Spend a few minutes to come up with something you can try alone and something to try with your children. How about encouraging your children to write or tell stories? Help them write a poem for Grandma. How about a craft project?

Make Barbie doll furniture out of boxes. An egg carton section makes a nice footstool. For creativity in the kitchen, let your children make smiley faces or animal features on fruit or sliced bread. Use raisins or pineapple with mayo for gluing food on other food. Carrot shreds and coconut make fun hair. Make sailboats and rafts out of bread and cheese. Thank God for creating all our colorful, richly textured, and nourishing foods as you create your own delicacies. If something turns out especially nice, you might encourage your children to repeat the creation for a family gathering.

Be silly, be imaginative, and have fun. Your son(s) as well as your daughter(s) will enjoy sharing in creative enterprises.

Exploring Scripture

Creation is such an important activity that the Bible begins and ends with it! Genesis 1:1 tells us, "In the beginning God created the heavens and the earth." And then Revelation 21:5 says, "then He who sat on the throne said, 'Behold, I make all things new.' And He said to me, 'Write, for these words are true and faithful.'"

Taking Action

- Releasing creativity is one of those areas where we simply have to do it before we can evaluate whether we have a creative bent. What creative activity would you like to try?

⁂

Lord, help me to take the time to do a little advance planning so that I'm ready to see the possibilities of things I can make in the world around me. Help me to think creatively and to share these ideas with my children. Keep me out of the rut of always doing things the same way.

Pleasing God

*I*t's natural to desire to please God, but we can come perilously close to drifting away from God because we feel we can never do enough to please Him.

Guess what? There's good news! God wants us to know that we are pleasing to Him as we are and that He delights in us! It's not what we *do* but what's been *done* by Jesus.

Wow! That means, among other things, that we can quit trying so hard to please God and can bask in being loved.

Kathie Lee has the right attitude. In a *Guideposts* article (January 1996) she says, "I've never felt apologetic about my faith or my career; it's the Lord I want to please, not critics or 'religious' people."

Some women are too intent on keeping the human beings in their lives happy to even think about pleasing God. Angie was an older woman going through change-of-life and given to bouts of depression. I was the fourth psychotherapist she consulted. Angie needed marriage counseling, but her husband refused. She also had a critical mother who was constantly nagging her. Angie needed to confront her mom, but she was afraid. Angie felt trapped until she fully surrendered responsibility for making her mother happy. Angie also had to quit focusing excessively on pleasing her husband despite his indifference to her. She put her personal priority on pleasing God. Finally, she found contentment.

Exploring Scripture

Psalm 16:3 says, "As for the saints who are on the earth, 'They are the excellent ones, in whom is all my delight.'"

• How does God's delight in us provide security?

James 4:7–8, 10 says, "Submit yourselves, then, to God. Resist the devil, and he will flee from you. Come near to God and he will come near to you. Wash your hands, you sinners, and purify your hearts, you double-minded. . . . Humble yourselves before the Lord, and He will lift you up" (NIV).

- What are some of the attitudes and actions that specifically please God?

Taking Action

If you have confessed your sins, asked God to fill your life, and you're trying to live by His Word, you are pleasing to God! Whatever your past, Jesus forgives. You're a plain, straight-out saint according to 1 Corinthians 1:2: "To the church of God in Corinth, to those sanctified in Christ Jesus and called to be holy, together with all those everywhere who call on the name of our Lord Jesus Christ—their Lord and ours" (NIV). This may sound shocking if you haven't considered it before. Sainthood doesn't necessarily involve doing miraculous things for God. It's what we presently are through the power of Christ.

- Think of some Christians you know that you recognize as saints right now on earth even in their human frailties and write their names here:

Your reading this book is evidence of your desire to please God. As you apply these principles, try this action, too. Just sit alone with your eyes closed and picture God as a Father. He's teaching you how to walk. He keeps encouraging you when you fall. Over and over He helps you back on your feet and heads you out in the right direction. He's already checked that there's no furniture in the way that could seriously hurt you. He knows you're not able to do it alone so He stands by ready to catch you. Pleasing God is easy. You just take your little steps and He watches, encourages, and delights in you. Remember this picture, replay it often. That's how pleased your Father is with you!

Dear Heavenly Father, please help me to keep my eyes on You and desire to please You foremost. Thank You for the specific encouragement You give me in Your Word. I love to experience Your love day by day.

TWENTY–SIX

Protecting Faith

Sooner or later our children will come in contact with other religious beliefs. Our children will hear that faith is a crutch for people who need an excuse for failure or insecurity. To the young, God may seem unnecessary. Postmidnight discussions at slumber parties in high school and in college dorms are fertile ground for loss of faith unless our children are well informed. Many young people lose their faith in God because they hear arguments that sound good but are false. We need to clothe our children with the spiritual truths that are the right size for their ages just as we clothe them with physical garments that fit.

Hosea 4:6 warns, "My people are destroyed for lack of knowledge." We and our children need to learn how to effectively counter arguments like "How can you believe that stuff?" "Why shove your beliefs on your children?" "Everybody's opinions and beliefs are as valid as everybody else's." "Religion is a cultural belief; culture changes." "Your faith is old-fashioned and outdated."

When asked what faith is, some people say it's believing what you know isn't true! Or believing what you can't know! Both those statements are false. Faith is a reasonable belief system. We need to get the facts about other religious beliefs and cults first and be prepared to answer questions. We must not be deceived; we must protect ourselves and our children. We can have a collection of books on hand to supply the answers we don't have. We'll be protecting our children as we're educating ourselves.

We must teach our children that belief in a personal God is relevant to their daily lives. Do your children think God keeps a scorecard and totals their good and bad deeds? I used to think that was true, and I wouldn't know until I got to heaven if I could get in or not. Faith is not a set of rules we follow to become good people.

Other faiths may contain part of the truth. Much doubt comes from ignorance of what Jesus actually said and did. For example, a friend told my husband and me when we were new Christians that he couldn't believe in Jesus because Jesus never claimed to be God. I nodded sympathetically, not knowing he was dead wrong until we began our own examination of Scripture.

We can make a strong historical case for the credibility of God's Word, the Bible, but the best proof is changed lives. Addicts get set free; men get touched by God and return to their families. Haven't we all seen people so close to Christ that their faces glowed when they spoke of Him? These are signs of His power among us still.

Exploring Scripture

Second Corinthians 10:5 says, "We demolish arguments and every pretension that sets itself up against the knowledge of God, and we take captive every thought to make it obedient to Christ" (NIV).

• What does this verse tell us to do to guard our faith?

How does God help us protect and share the faith? In 1 John 5:13 we read, "These things I have written . . . that you may *know* . . ." and in Philippians 2:13 we read, ". . . it is God who works in you both to will and do for His good pleasure." God wants His children to know Him and has given the Bible as a source of truth. What a relief to have God working in us to help us keep and share our faith!

Taking Action

Role play with someone who will take the role of a nonbeliever. Practice until you can respond to their objections clearly. Use Scripture to back up your statements. Have your children practice until they're comfortable explaining their beliefs.

For further study read *Surprised by Faith* by Don Bierle; *Mere Christianity* by C. S. Lewis, and *Evidence That Demands a Verdict* by Josh McDowell, and discuss these books with your children. Being well prepared is our best defense against the attacks that will inevitably come to our faith.

❦

Lord, there will always be those who do not love You and who seek to destroy our faith in You. Keep me studying Your Word diligently. Give me knowledge and understanding of You and Your Word, both for myself and for teaching Your truths to my children.

TWENTY–SEVEN

Celebrating Often

Fifty-year-old Wanda seemed to exist in a web of routine broken only by interruptions required by the needs of her children or friends. She'd worked hard as a child and never expected to do less as an adult. She liked always having some chore just ahead that demanded her attention.

As a child, Wanda had never gone out much or been encouraged to get involved in outside activities. In fact her nervous, fearful mother acted as if something horrible would happen to Wanda when she went out. It was easier for Wanda to stay home than deal with her mother's tension.

After she married, Wanda lived near her parents' home. At first Wanda's husband tried to get her enthused about his sports interests. He eventually gave up. She thought money spent on recreation was frivolous. She seldom called friends. They were probably just as busy as she was and wouldn't want to be disturbed. And she rarely entertained because of the extra work and expense.

Wanda wasn't much fun to be around, and her husband and two children often left her home alone. She didn't mind; she could get more done without them around. When Wanda had some spare time, she'd tackle some extra household project and then complain about her drudgery.

In the biblical story of the Prodigal Son in Luke 15, we find a joyless elder brother—he may have been a lot like Wanda. Although the story focuses on the younger son and the father's joy when the son repents of his wrong ways and returns home, the father's elder son wasn't thrilled to see his disobedient younger brother being treated like royalty. The elder son had plodded along day by day being the good guy, probably priding himself on his faithful diligence. Do you get the impression that the eldest's lifestyle must have been a drudge?

Why was it unusual for the elder son to hear music and dancing coming from his house? Whose fault was it the elder son hadn't often had parties there for his friends?

Was he upset because he never stopped to enjoy the benefits he had?

The dad, who symbolizes God in the story, says to the elder son, "Everything I have is yours." All he had to do was ask.

📖 Exploring Scripture

Luke 15:28–31 in Phillips' translation reads, "Then he [the elder son] burst out: 'Look, how many years have I slaved for you and never disobeyed a single order of yours, and yet you have never given me so much as a young goat, so that I could give my friends a dinner! But when that son of yours arrives, who has spent all your money on prostitutes, for *him* you kill the calf we've fattended!' But the father replied: 'My dear son, you have been with me all the time and everything I have is yours.'"

- What can we learn about the lifestyle and expectations of the "good" older son?

- The dad says in verse 32: "We *had* to celebrate and show our joy." When was the last time you celebrated your joy?

- Does your life indicate that you know how to celebrate the blessings in your life?

📝 Taking Action
- If you're not having good times regularly, what keeps you from celebrating joyfully with your husband and with your family?

- Check off which attitudes apply to you (and which attitudes you're giving your children):

  ___ 1. You feel guilty when you're not productive.

  ___ 2. You feel like you don't deserve special times.

  ___ 3. You feel convinced you can't afford to have fun.

  ___ 4. You feel it's wrong to spend money for frivolity.

  ___ 5. You feel fun is a waste of time.

  ___ 6. You're drifting through your days, not planning ahead.

  ___ 7. You're lazy about following through on arrangements.

  ___ 8. You expect others to make suggestions and plans for you.

  ___ 9. You're bitter that others seem to have more fun than you.

  ___ 10. There's nothing to celebrate.

- Ask God what's holding you back from celebrating more often and enjoying your life more. Is it something within you or within your circumstances? Are there any attitudes mentioned earlier that you need to change?

❧❧❧

Father, You have given us work to do to be productive for You, but You have also given us many reasons to celebrate. Give me a grateful heart to celebrate the joys You freely give. Free me from the routine of drudgery and make my spirit joyful and happy.

TWENTY-EIGHT

Being Real

*T*amara met a woman who told her, "We probably don't have much in common; you have so much faith. My husband and I are pretty discouraged, and our life is full of problems, some of which are our fault." Tamara wondered, "What kind of image am I projecting? Some super-religious, perfect specimen no one can identify with?"

One of Pamela's neighbors said to her, "We enjoy being with you. Many people at church are so superficial. When we're with them, we feel our family isn't perfect enough. And we're uncomfortable because we don't know the Bible that well either."

We're all imperfect humans. We sin and need to repent frequently; we all need lots of encouragement to grow as Christians.

When Jesus was around other people, He didn't intimidate them. Many people thought He was a neat guy and probably said, "Let's invite Jesus because He's fun to talk with and tells neat stories," or "Let's ask Him another question and see what He thinks." People could be comfortable around Jesus; they knew He was for real.

At the same time, Jesus didn't hide what was most important to Him. He just didn't make a big deal out of it. When he went off alone to pray, He didn't say, "It's been a nice party; now you guys all come out to the hills with me for some prayer time." He simply did what was important to him without flaunting or fanfare. And the people got curious. Jesus didn't nag or pester. He said to the rich young ruler, "OK, you asked what you do to get into the kingdom and I've answered you, but the choice is yours."

And Jesus' relationship with His Father was so special, nothing interfered with it. Do we wake up each morning saying, "I can't wait to talk to the Father! Another day to praise the Lord and serve Him"? Is that our attitude toward life? Or do we call ourselves Christians and then go about our lives as if Jesus didn't matter at all?

If our relationship with God is so important, why aren't we all doing more about it? We can't live for the Kingdom that begins on earth unless we're willing to mingle with people. It's scary to be real, because we can no longer be phony. We're one of the bunch on the front line with the other real people struggling with confusion and sinfulness. We can be strong enough spiritually and emotionally to be real only if we keep our relationship with the Father supertight.

All God's people are sinners as well as saints. He loves us extravagantly—enough to die for all. I have some good friends and pleasant business acquaintances who are homosexual. I certainly enjoy their creativity, their wit, and their kindnesses. They know I'm a Christian and are rather confused that I like them—and they find me likable. I've had several opportunities to share my faith with them. But I avoid compromising social situations where I could get into a position of appearing to promote their lifestyle.

Over the years I've found that after I've formed a friendly relationship with someone and presented God's truth in a loving way, if my friend chooses to remain in a sinful lifestyle, I often move on to other friendships, but I try to keep the doors open. I excuse myself from frequent companionship. By staying in close contact with the Father, I've found Him to be faithful in letting me know when to back off and when to offer friendship.

Intimacy means "In To Me See." If we will admit our faults to others, they can know who we really are—imperfect people who want to improve. Jesus knew this. Scripture recommends confessing our sins to one another. If we're willing to give up the pretense of perfection, people around us can show us their true images.

📖 Exploring Scripture

The Phillips translation describes Jesus' intense feelings in Mark 14:33–34 as follows: "He took with Him Peter, James and John and began to be horror-stricken and desperately depressed. 'My heart is nearly breaking,' he told them."

Can you identify with this image of our Lord? It's real. Jesus wasn't afraid to share feelings—angry, sad, rejected, disappointed, and betrayed by His close friend. Jesus felt it and showed it. He survived these emotions by turning to His Father in heaven. Over and over I teach counseling clients to do exactly this. Feel your emotions deeply, then move on. Don't get stuck in them.

Look up Luke 7:36–50. Jesus was invited to have dinner with Simon, a Pharisee, one of the guys investigating who Jesus was. Jesus went. It was a chance to reach Simon. While there, Jesus allowed a woman who was a known sinner to wash His feet, a woman who shouldn't be touching a holy man. Jesus straightened Simon out when Simon was surprised. Jesus came to save sinners.

✒ *Taking Action*

- Who are the sinners yet to be saved by grace that you spend time with?

- When you're with them, do they know you're really like them except for the righteousness Christ gave you?

- If you befriended an alcoholic, a prostitute, or a homosexual, how would that go over at your church?

❦

Heavenly Father, You know me as no person on earth knows me. You see me with all the gifts and talents You've given me, and You see me struggle with sin and doubt. Help me to be open with those around me, that my life will lead others to You because they see the honesty and freshness that only You can give.

TWENTY NINE

Refreshing Yourself

ealing with physical weariness is difficult, but we all know what we need to do—get extra rest, reduce stressful demands, adjust our schedules. But handling emotional and spiritual weariness can be more difficult.

A client struggled with being disciplined in prayer and Bible study. In sharing her faith with her brother and sister-in-law they said, "We're glad you found something that means so much to you, but we're happy with our life the way it is." Her relatives were carefree, traveling in their free time and even occasionally helping others, not as an act of service in Christ but simply as a nice thing to do. My client concluded people can be fulfilled without God and began questioning the "Lord stuff" in her life.

Can people be fulfilled without Christ? Yes and no. Perhaps temporarily, but not eternally. Consider these issues:

1. Are non-Christians as happy as they profess? Some people wear a mask. In counseling I often glimpse confusion and pain behind the smiling facade.
2. No one wishes misfortune upon another person, but trials do come. Sometimes a house of seeming happiness is built on sand. The house may look great, but adversity may prove it isn't. Jesus warned about building on shifting sand.
3. Non-Christians can be happy, but would they be happier still if they knew the God of the universe?

It's natural for us to want an answer for non-Christians' apparent success and satisfaction. We want non-Christian friends and relatives to have happiness, but we're confused when they seem so content or successful while we struggle at times.

How can we refresh ourselves spiritually? What helps me most to refresh myself is my Scripture arsenal. We all need at least one, maybe two or three, awesome verses. We can memorize the words so we carry them with us wherever we go. We can whisper them into our hearts when we're in difficult situations. Somehow the Word is like an injection of nitroglycerin—fast-acting, recharging, refocusing. God's Word works! When we just want a minute alone and can't get one, we can go into the privacy of our own mind.

When we have time for a longer pick-me-up, we can read Psalms. As we meditate on the words the psalmist used to describe almighty God, we can pick something poetic, practical, striking, forceful—whatever appeals to us and gives us an image of God that we like to think about.

We can fall asleep at night repeating a verse to ourselves and thinking about its meaning. Using a special verse calms us when we're driving through stalled traffic or when we're waiting in line with groceries for dinner. A special verse for our morning prayers helps us drag ourselves out of bed.

Most of us already know that it's helpful when we're going though any time of trial to see what God's Word says about His help, His presence, and His support. But how many of us run there first? Sound too simple, too naive? People I counsel through grief, financial distress, or rebellion of a child are intensely comforted by memorizing a Scripture verse that fits their situation.

Scripture reminds us often to speak the Word and meditate on the Word. Why? God knows His Word. He doesn't need to hear us say it. But we need to bask in it, like soul sunshine.

Exploring Scripture

Morning, noon, and night, refresh yourself in God's Word. Make up your own collection of Scripture treasures. Women have a heart-chord for beauty. You can surround yourself with beautiful thoughts and exquisite ideas, whatever your budget! The "furniture" in the private room of your mind can be as fine as any Queen's or First Lady's!

Here are some possibilities. Pick your favorite "soul sunshine."

- "May the favor of the LORD our God rest upon us; establish the work of our hands for us—yes, establish the work of our hands" (Psalm 90:17 NIV). Believe me, that's a great mind-setter for starting a day!
- "He who dwells in the shelter of the Most High will rest in the shadow of the Almighty. I will say of the LORD, 'He is my refuge and my fortress, my God, in whom I trust'" (Psalm 91:1–2 NIV). This is a great help for going through the day.
- "Praise the LORD, O my soul; all my inmost being, praise his holy name. Praise the LORD, O my soul, and forget not all his benefits" (Psalm 103:1–2 NIV). What a way to fall asleep at night! Start

listing all His benefits and blessings one by one, and you'll be asleep before you can finish.

Remind yourself that if you go by God's clock, you'll never become impatient. "For a thousand years in your sight are like a day that has just gone by, or like a watch in the night" (Psalm 90:4). So what's a day like?

Taking Action

Memorize one verse per day or one a week—medical research confirms the physical benefit of using our minds to keep them sharp and clear. Why should that be surprising? Using every part of the body keeps it healthy. There are a lot of dull minds running around in healthy bodies. I see many women for counseling who have eliminated time to think and time to pray from their lives because of their crammed schedules, and they are emotionally and spiritually exhausted.

- What circumstances are making you spiritually weary?

- Select one verse that you will commit to memorize and use as a lift to your spirits, one that will be hidden in your heart for just such a time, and write it here:

❧

Lord, Your Word refreshes my spirit. Your truth, Your encouragement feeds me. The weariness and baggage of this life fall away, and I am renewed.

THIRTY

Surviving Your Husband's Life Crises

*W*hat is commonly called a male midlife crisis can occur at any age and at any time to Christians as well as non-Christians. Some men seem to hit a crisis every month when they pay the bills. Some men hit a crisis after about seven years of marriage; others, when they have a milestone birthday like forty or fifty. A specific item like the loss of a job may trigger the crisis, or it may come from a subtle buildup over time when a man sees himself growing older without having realized his dreams. Sometimes the entrance of an attractive, available woman in the work environment makes a man question his priorities.

A client named Paul is typical of men entering a crisis. Paul saw routine settling over his life when he turned fifty. The desires he had for extraordinary success were evaporating. A vague sense of uneasiness settled over him.

Here are some of the signs of a man in midlife crisis. Some men go into a mild depression that may be brief or may deepen until professional help is needed. Some men try to be a kid again. Don't get me wrong— not all men who buy motorcycles do so because they're undergoing emotional turmoil, but some do. I've seen professional men decide to grow their hair ponytail length. Others start exercising their bodies because that waistline that stayed trim without any effort is starting to look more and more like their dad's.

The most frightening and dangerous midlife crisis occurs when a husband seeks another woman to add some excitement to his life and nurture his ego. I wish this never happened, but it does. I advise wives not to live in the fear of losing their husbands, but to take practical steps to keep their husband's love. It's like keeping the house boarded up against a hurricane because a hurricane is what divorce is like for the rejected party. Many women have said they would have rather died than have gone through this pain. It's particularly hard when infidelity is totally unsuspected.

Our husbands have free wills and can choose to sin or not to sin. We may do all the right things as wives and still end up in divorce court. But, of course, we want to make sure we haven't unknowingly contributed to infidelity. A husband's crisis is probably not caused by his wife, but it's often easy for him to find a cause outside himself like his wife, his children, or his job.

Let me share what usually happens in a husband's crisis. The wife becomes bitter and angry which only justifies her husband's thoughts that she's a nag. How could he ever have married her? He was too young and immature. His new girlfriend never yells; she keeps telling him how great he is. Then the wife tries to turn the children against their father—and his attention toward them becomes less and less.

Married men are increasingly leaving their family responsibilities for other women or for the single life. Some are even experimenting with homosexuality for the happiness they're not finding in traditional family life. These men have never known a vital, exciting Christian family. They need teaching from God's Word. Promise Keepers is one organization giving men a right understanding of their personal dignity and their need to lead a godly family. Undoubtedly that's why it's being attacked vigorously by the ungodly in our society.

Sometimes it's the wife who wants to leave the marriage. Don't. Wives need to get help to make the marriage as good as possible. Maybe it will never be perfect, but marriage is a commitment made before God until death, and God honors us for keeping our commitments. Our children will call us blessed for staying with their fathers and making sure their fathers remain part of their lives.

Men abuse their wives for many reasons, although alcohol and other drugs are often the culprit. But in some cases, wives are also a part of the cycle of violence. With her words a woman can devastate a man emotionally. Not every case of wife abuse starts this way, don't get me wrong, but I've seen too many not to mention it. As wives we must guard both our mouths and our own actions.

📖 *Exploring Scripture*

What does Proverbs 14:1 say about a wise woman? "The wise woman builds her house, but the foolish pulls it down with her hands."

- In what ways have you built your house up?
- In what ways might you be pulling it down with your own hands?

Psalm 141:3 says, "Set a guard, O LORD, over my mouth; keep watch over the door of my lips."

- In what ways are you using your mouth to build up your husband and your marriage?

- Are there any specific areas where you need to make sure the Lord is guarding your mouth?

Taking Action

If your husband has an affair, go to God before you go to a lawyer. Pray and listen to God—not your husband, family, or friends. Fighting to save your husband from throwing away your marriage will be like riding a bucking bronco—he'll try to buck you off, but hang on.

How? Think of him as sick. You wouldn't abandon him if he had cancer. Your husband is spiritually sick. If he had a healthy relationship with God, your husband wouldn't be succumbing to temptation outside his marriage. You're not the problem. Don't let his criticism of you make you respond in kind. Show him extra signs of your love. Work out your anger with God and with a friend or counselor who doesn't believe in divorce and will help you move into a state of forgiveness. This is crucial if there's to be a future reconciliation, but it's also critical for your own spiritual health.

Let your husband know you still love him and want his affection back. Be tender and kind. But don't act desperate and don't submit to physical abuse; that can lower his respect for you. You need to wait and pray and be willing to take your husband back in forgiveness. This solution can work, but it's probably the hardest thing you'll ever do. You have to believe what God says about the sanctity and indissolubility of marriage to be willing to surrender false pride and righteous anger. If he still insists on leaving, let him go, knowing he may yet come back.

If he returns and is reconciled to God and you, your marriage will be enriched as well as saved. Your relationship will be incredible because your husband will personally have experienced the love of God the Father, Jesus, and the Holy Spirit through you.

If your husband shares his feelings readily, continue to be his sounding block, the safe place where he can talk out his successes and his disappointments. If your husband is on the quiet side, be his frequent companion. Be an encouragement to him.

Remember when you were dating and you couldn't wait to be with him? And you spent time thinking about what you were going to say to one another? Make that part of your married life too. Make sure you don't put your children before your husband. Kids will usually clamor for attention and take all that you're willing to give. There must be limits like saying, "It's nine o'clock; Dad and I need for you to go to your room and read, study, or chat on the phone with a friend. This is our private time to talk or watch TV together or go out for a walk."

You can help your husband survive crises by making him feel special in little and big ways. Make his favorite meal or make a big deal of going to his favorite restaurant sometimes. When my kids were little and I was at home with them, we straightened up the house before Dad came home to make his homecoming seem special. Maybe your husband gets there first and does that for you. Tell him that you appreciate what he does for the family.

Lord, I know life is not easy for my husband. Teach me daily how to show him love and how to help him in the rough places. Teach me patience and tenderness and to watch my tongue when I speak to him. Help me to always remember that he is a precious gift from You.

Focusing on God

We can call it prayer, meditation, whatever word we choose, but what does it take to get our heads and our hearts focused on God? I've asked lots of women this question. Their answers may help us find new ways to give more attention to God in our everyday lives.

Kathy walks every morning and holds a silent conversation with the Lord. Often she uses an alphabet game to stimulate her thoughts. Here's how it works: Kathy chooses any letter, like "K" for example, and thinks of words related to God that begin with that letter (or she goes through the alphabet in order). When she came to "Z" she thought of the zenith, the highest point; zoom, God goes right to the heart; and zig-zag, God works in mysterious ways.

Caryl goes out to jog and listens to a praise music tape to get her mind and heart elevated above her surroundings.

Terry likes to do something with her hands, like gardening, while she prays. She makes sure she doesn't become more involved in the process of what she's doing than thinking about God.

Connie framed pictures with Scripture verses for wall decorations in her home. She likes to sit in her favorite chair and let her thoughts dwell on Jesus as she looks around. Like an art museum displays paintings, Connie uses Scripture displays.

My friend Angela needs to read something and use the written word as a bridge to cross over into her own deeper thought processes.

Pat thrives on hearing how God has helped others. She never misses her two weekly sharing groups with some Christian friends because that strengthens her relationship with God and her dependence on Him too.

Each of these women is refreshed by experiencing God in her own unique way, and each one of us needs to find the way that most directly ministers to us personally.

A question to ask ourselves is "Do I respond better to messages I receive through my eyes, through my ears, or through my hands?" Throughout the day we're involved in using all three senses, but which helps us most to direct our thoughts to God?

Whatever it takes, find it and repeat it over and over. We can build these opportunities for focusing on God into our everyday lives, so that it's natural to spend time thinking on Him.

I personally am helped by both visual and auditory reminders. When I decorate or need to make a clothing choice, I choose things to remind me of God. For example, I selected a pattern of three geometric shapes on my floor tile to prod my thoughts of the Father, Son, and Holy Spirit. My ranch house happens to be laid out in the shape of a cross. I flip on the tape recorder which is always preset to my favorite music. It sets my frame of mind for prayer and becomes a transition from what I've been doing.

Our goal is to be God-focused in everything we do, but that takes practice. At first we need to be content with simply extending the time that we set aside to specifically focus on Him.*

Exploring Scripture

Read Joshua 4. Symbols were an important tool God used so that His message would not be forgotten. Can you find a scriptural example of a symbol like stones being used in the Old Testament as reminders?

Taking Action

- For your prayer time this week, experiment with a "focusing on God" activity involving seeing or hearing. Which sense best helps you to concentrate on our Lord?

Surround me with Your presence, Lord, so that I see You everywhere. Thank You for art and music that fill me with sights and sounds of You and keep my mind on Your thoughts and Your ways.

---

* *Experiencing God* by Henry Blackaby and Claude King (Nashville: Broadman and Holman, 1994) is a wonderful encouragement for increasing your intimacy with God. *My Utmost for His Highest* by Oswald Chambers will help your love for God deepen.

Leading Others to Christ

*L*etting the light of Christ in our lives shine the way to Him— that's what leading others to Christ is about. I count it my greatest delight to know Christ and lead someone to Him. Nothing is as satisfying as knowing I've helped lead someone else to this incredible joy.

Although we want to lead others to Christ and we realize it's also God's command, we may sometimes have hesitations. The most common concerns I hear women express are

- "I'm frightened at the thought of the awesome responsibility. What if I mess up? This person might be lost forever."

  That's not true. God will use us, but He does not depend on us alone to accomplish His purpose. We may be the person who gets the soul ready; our role may be to get a person thinking or asking questions. Or we may even confuse other persons or disturb them which can lead to their seeking answers elsewhere.

- "I hate to bring up such a controversial subject."

  Sometimes we're afraid that we'll be ridiculed. Nobody likes that feeling. We sense that talking about Christ is risky because He's not everyday conversation in our culture. Yes, it's more comfortable to stay in the background and not risk somebody's disapproval, but obviously that didn't bother the early disciples and it must not bother us.

- "I don't know enough to counter any objections a nonbeliever may have."

  We probably can't answer every person's questions to their complete satisfaction. But in John 16:8 Jesus said about the work of the Holy Spirit, "And when He has come, He will convict the world of sin, and of righteousness, and of judgment." It isn't our job to convict people of their need of Christ; the Holy Spirit does that work. Our role is to focus our talk on Jesus Christ, His Gospel, and the Holy Spirit because these are the sources of change. The Gospel ". . . is the power of God to salvation for everyone who believes" (Romans 1:16). We simply give information and ask questions like "What do you think?"

- "I'm sensitive to personal rejection if my friend doesn't want to believe."

  We can point out clearly why others should believe the Christian faith, yet some will still choose not to believe. If we receive a hostile reaction to our efforts, remember that may be the work of Satan who doesn't want this person to know Christ. We can't take it as a personal rejection of us, but of Christ. He can deal with rejection better than we can. Many people who later received Christ often share how someone "annoyed" them with their polite persistence.

- "Should I intrude with my own beliefs? What right do we have to discuss something this personal with another individual?"

  We can overcome this hesitation by thinking of the alternative. Do we believe hell is real? What would we do to keep this person from being destroyed? If we could reach out our hands right now to keep them from physical danger, would we? If we can save them from eternal spiritual and physical agony, won't we try?

- "What do I say, and how do I say it?"

  This is where we rely on our study, our effort, and God's power. Acts 1:8 is wonderful witnessing encouragement. "But you shall receive power when the Holy Spirit has come upon you; and you shall be witnesses to Me in Jerusalem, and in all Judea and Samaria, and to the ends of the earth."

Exploring Scripture

Everybody's got questions; you need to have answers. I like to use 2 Corinthians 5:14–15, 17: "For the love of Christ compels us, because we judge thus: that if One died for all, then all died; and He died for all, that those who live should live no longer for themselves, but for Him who died for them and rose again. . . . Therefore, if anyone is in Christ, he is a new creation; old things have passed away; behold, all things have become new." In a sense Paul was writing a guidebook in his letters. It might be called *How a Christian Leads Others to Christ.* He said to follow his example (modeled on the teachings of Jesus).

Taking Action

Sharing our faith isn't a task to perform; It comes naturally as we live and move about. It's unpredictable and exciting.

Two key elements in testifying for Christ are explaining what Jesus did for you on the cross personally and then relating how Christ has changed your own life. Stress to a nonbeliever that the Bible will teach you every significant truth that you need to live and to grow in Christ.

I've been privileged several times to be the person who hands the flower to Jesus, "Here's another beauty for Your Kingdom, Lord." I've heard people, young and old, pray and accept Christ—in places as varied as flying in an airplane or lying on a death bed.

Think of the world as God's garden. We Christians all assume different roles in the garden from time to time. Sometimes I am the flower soaking up the sun, and that's all I can do. Sometimes I provide the nutrients for the soil. Now and then I am the soil, like peat for a new plant until it's big and strong enough to be planted outside. Sometimes I'm the gardener fertilizing the plants to strengthen their stems and roots. Occasionally I get to revive a Christian flower that's almost dead. And I even go through seasons where I drop seeds and multiply! And God's garden becomes ever more gorgeous.

- How have others encouraged your own growth?

- What role(s) have you played thus far—a new plant in peat, a new bud, an open flower, a little straggly plant in need of fertilizer, the person who fertilizes the soil for others? Where do you see yourself?

- How can you better equip yourself to lead others to Christ?

Lord, I love bringing others into Your garden. I love working in Your garden, tending Your plants, in whatever role You have for me. Thank You for the privilege of leading others to You.

Enhancing Sexuality

A book for women isn't complete without discussing sexuality. Sexual intimacy gives a woman and her husband a sense of elation and completion that is not offered by any other circumstance of life. It is one of God's most precious gifts.

In marriage counseling I see the pain that comes from not understanding the role of sex. I know it seems amazing, but in counseling I still have to convince women of the value of sex. Sex is extraordinarily important to the majority of men, and lustful temptations aimed especially at men are everywhere. (I'd estimate well over fifty percent of all husbands deal with regular temptations toward lust.) When sex is freely alluded to in the actions, words, and dressing habits of people around us and acted out in television, movies, and advertising, it's a constant challenge to guard our own thoughts and actions against lustful temptations.

Most Christian men and women handle these temptations quite well, despite the fact that the sex drive is strong. In counseling women, furthermore, I always encourage them to make sure that their husbands are properly loved sexually and that they continue to find ways to have fun with their husbands in and out of bed. Sexual unfulfillment is a fertile ground for Satan's work, and many wives, without knowing it, help Satan.

The lessening of marital sexual intimacy is one of the problems in Christian culture now. The biggest causes aren't surprising—late-night TV, women preoccupied with work outside the home, and both men and women exhausted after a busy day.

So, how can women enhance sexual love in marriage today? Here are some tips.

- If possible, cut back on your hours at work or quit entirely.

    A woman's energy can be drained by the demands of her job in or out of the home. When a working mom with small children finally falls into bed at night, she wants to be left alone—with no more requests on her from anyone. Often she's simply not interested in anything physical. I suggest to my clients that if they work outside the home in a role that depletes them, it's essential to cut back their hours or quit if they possibly can.

- Don't be your husband's "mother."

  Carol's husband was proud of her authoritative role at work and the way she managed the children. But she wasn't his mother, and he didn't appreciate being bossed, corrected, or ridiculed by her. I had to help Carol readjust the way she related to her husband to improve their sex life. No healthy male wants to have sex with his "mother." A woman can help her husband become a lover again by finding some things about him to sincerely praise and bragging about him!

- Openly encourage emotional intimacy with your husband.

  Husbands need to know it's important to their wives not to feel used but to feel treasured. Before becoming physically intimate, a wife can ask her husband what he most loved about her that day. His words can create the emotional intimacy she needs to proceed.

- Reframe old, negative pictures.

  Christian women can be highly moral and fully sexual. Even if sexual abuse existed during childhood, women can have enjoyable sex with their husbands. Psychotherapists use a technique called "reframing" to help people with this issue. That means putting a different mental picture frame around an old print to make it suitable for now. The past was another time, another place. Women need to feel the pain, talk it through with someone they can trust, let go of the pain, and then determine not to let the past frame the new picture of life now.

- Enjoy the therapeutic aspects of sex.

  Sex has many benefits, too! The September 1995 *Reader's Digest* reports that sex enhances the immune system, reduces chronic pain by stimulating the immune system, and reduces stress through its natural sedative properties. It further states that sex is perhaps the best preventive and healing medicine there is!

Your sexual activities are a personal topic. Keep the sexual relationship between you and your husband a private matter. Your sex life is one of the few areas of discussion in which openness with outsiders is not appropriate.

If you don't enjoy sex, go to a counselor of your same sex to discuss deeper causes of your dissatisfaction. I believe that women should avoid discussing sexuality issues with their pastor or even a professional male counselor. If you don't have a sexual interest in your husband, someone else will. This is critical.

What can you do to enhance your sexuality? Try these tips:

1. Remind yourself that sex is God's gift to you for physical joy, and you can enjoy sex even if you've been raped, abused, or taught that it's a forbidden act. Focus on sex as God's plan, His design for you as a woman.

2. Plan for sexual dates with your husband. Don't wait until bedtime. Slip away to the bathroom, a walk-in closet, or lock the door of your room and tell your children not to disturb you for a half hour.

3. Be creatively romantic. Women often complain that their husbands aren't romantic enough, but they've stopped hanging onto his arm. Sit on his lap occasionally. Reach out and hold his hand when you're walking side by side. If you think your husband isn't still flattered by your sweet words and your physical attention, ask him. You'll be surprised.

4. Discuss sex freely with your husband. Look at him, admire him. Remind him that you still find him very sexually attractive. Someone else will if you don't. Sadly, some men are attracted to adultery because their wives seldom affirmed their sexuality or verbally and physically expressed their enjoyment of their husband's sexuality.

5. If one of you must travel in your work, try to keep it minimal. Plan special farewells and return celebrations.

6. If your efforts don't get the response you'd like remember, there *are* men who could care less about sex. Some have been sexually wounded and are afraid of sexual intimacy. If that's your husband, encourage him to seek help from your pastor or a respected Christian counselor.

7. Break the routine of your married life. Meet for lunch or go out for coffee and dessert at night. On these minidates here's an activity I call an IR—Intimacy Reviver—that will promote your emotional intimacy, the rich soil for physical love:

   - Discuss your moment closest to God. (God is the source of all love.)
   - Share the moment you felt closest to one another.
   - Tell when you were proudest of one another.
   - Describe the nicest thing each of you did for the other that week.
   - Speak only in positives, allow no negative comments.

You're involved in activities during the week that draw you and your husband apart. For one to two hours draw back together like a rubber band returning to its original shape. Why does this work? You make each other feel good when you share a proud moment and affirm each other.

 ## Exploring Scripture

- Read Proverbs 5:15–23. What are the instructions regarding sex?

Notice enjoying your spouse comes *before* the warnings about engaging in an adulterous affair. If you are sharing the pleasures of sexual intimacy with your spouse, running to anyone else's arms is unnecessary. Remember, God sees and ponders all.

There's a command here: Be satisfied with your own mate at all times! Let your head and your heart be busy planning ways to enjoy intimate times with your husband, and you won't get into trouble. Don't be like Karen, a woman who didn't withhold sex but she may as well have. Her reluctance was obvious. She didn't realize how demeaning that was to her husband. She knew 1 Corinthians 7:4, "The wife's body does not belong to her alone but also to her husband. In the same way, the husband's body does not belong to him alone but also to his wife" (NIV). She needed to add love and affection to what she considered an obligation.

 ## Taking Action

- There are many wonderful books and tapes with suggestions for showing physical love. Among the most helpful are *The Act of Marriage* by Tim and Beverly LaHaye (Grand Rapids: Zondervan, 1976) and *Intended for Pleasure: Sex Tecniques and Sexual Fulfillment in Christian Marriage* by Ed and Gaye Wheat (Grand Rapids: Baker, 1979). Excellent audio tapes by Ed Wheat are also available—"Love-Life, Tapes I and II" and "Sex Techniques in Marriage." Listen to these tapes together at home, and discuss what you've heard. Remember, romance starts at breakfast and remind your husband that it works both ways. Keep a perfume bottle on the kitchen window sill.

- What else can you do to encourage sexual intimacy in your marriage?

- Encourage your husband to find as much joy in satisfying you as himself. Don't be shy about telling him what you would like and experimenting. Find satisfaction in pleasing him, too.

Lord, help me each day to look at my husband as Your gift to me. Help me to cherish him and love him as You planned for us. Help me see ways I can please him sexually and stay close to him as both a lover and a friend.

Guarding Your Church

*W*hile counseling clients within the church and working with pastors of various denominations, I often hear stories of dissension about doctrines and ministries within a church. This dissension can occur when a few people begin to advocate a certain way of doing things and prod other church members to follow them until everyone is forced to take sides.

Dissension ultimately destroys the strength of the unified church. The issue that divides can be a basic doctrinal tenet or a concern with a particular behavior. Just last week I heard of a church conflict because a missionary came back from Africa on sabbatical and began moving exuberantly in their church during services as the worshipers do in Africa. Those opposed felt so strongly against this (they considered it dancing) that they chose to leave the church when the pastor didn't see fit to confront the missionary.

In contrast we read in Acts 15:28–29 how sensitive the early apostles were to avoiding splits over the circumcision of the Gentiles. Paul said, "For it has seemed right to the Holy Spirit and to us to lay no further burden upon you except what is absolutely essential, namely, that you avoid what has been sacrificed to idols, tasting blood, eating the meat of what has been strangled, and sexual immorality. Keep yourselves clear of these things and you will make good progress" (PHILLIPS).

Such tender concern! Such loving acceptance! This is what we are all called to practice. But there's a sham going on in some hearts that God will not tolerate within His church body.

Is your church focusing more on reaching sinners or promoting unnecessary doctrinal tenets? We must keep straight the difference between what's important and what's minor, between hating the sin and welcoming the sinner.

Jesus went to the cross without yelling, criticizing, or complaining about the lousy sinners who made His death necessary. Instead He made the most compassionate statement ever spoken, "Father, forgive them, they do not know what they do" (Luke 23:34). Do we truly believe that? When people sin, do they know what they do? In that one moment of action, they made a choice. But do they know what consequences of that act they're bringing upon themselves and their families from that decision? Of course not.

False righteousness is the sin that made Jesus furious. His strongest language was spoken to those whitened sepulchers who acted so pure on the outside. Jesus saw into hearts and He proclaimed there's nobody, not a man or woman, who has never sinned. We need to open up our church doors as well as our arms to embrace those who are dealing with sin and tell them about Jesus.

Isn't Jesus warning us today too? We must not guard our churches from the sinner. Part of the church He came and cleansed has fallen into rigid righteousness again. I know that's true because I've counseled divorced people who have felt only partially accepted by their churches. Some churches will not allow them to be in a position of ministry.

I've heard painful stories from individuals with AIDS who receive more love and compassion from the gay community than they do from the church community. We need a balance between hating evil and loving people. Loving people always comes first. We Christians must be cautious not to become the new hypocrites.

Jesus warned the devout religious people of His day of the huge danger of hypocrisy—preaching love but becoming obsessed with "our doctrinal position." When someone sins and repents, do the church members act as if the sin is buried in the depths of the ocean?

Sometimes righteousness is simply a disguise for fear. Fear gets in the way of love. What do the nurses who minister to the sick and dying with Mother Teresa do with their fears? Do you think the good Samaritan might have had to overcome some fear that the robbers would return and finish him off too? Or that this guy he was helping might end up dependent on him for months? But the Samaritan ignored fear and ministered to the person attacked by robbers.

Taste the sweetness of love. Once we've ministered to hurting lives, the joy erases our selfishness and fear. In that instant we know it's true what Jesus says, "You're doing it for me" (Matt. 25:40).

I once had poison oak and looked awful. I can't begin to express the pain I felt when people avoided me and wouldn't come near, let alone touch me. I could read it in the way they'd sidle away and avert their eyes as much as possible. It was humiliating. I remember that when I minister to others now.

Pray for God's protection and love; take precaution and then get involved. We can't let our churches die because members are more concerned with finding others who share their ideology than with sharing the love of Christ with hurting people.

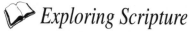 *Exploring Scripture*

Look up Phillipians 2:3: "Let nothing be done through selfish ambition or conceit but in lowliness of mind—let each esteem others better than himself." If everyone in the church body practiced this principle, we would not have dissension in the church.

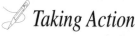 *Taking Action*

- Do the words that Jesus used for the "church" people of His day apply to my church? What does my church need to do to show more love to the outside world?

- What can I do to love my fellow church member as Jesus commanded?

The Christian classic *In His Steps* by Charles Sheldon talks about a church community that made a commitment to make every decision as Christ would for a specified period of time. The experiment changed their lives. Would your church be willing to try this experiment? For further application, read *The Body* by Chuck Colson.

❧❦❧

Heavenly Father, I long to love others as You love them, to see others as You see them. Make me into a person who strengthens my church with love, acceptance, and prayer for both the members and those who have recently come to worship with us.

THIRTY–FIVE

Balancing Effortlessly

As a child, did you ever try to walk along a beam as you swayed from one side to the other? You probably had to swing your arms rapidly to pull back to the middle, and then you regained your balance until suddenly you started to slip this way and that again.

Being a wife, mother, and working woman is also a challenging balancing act. I've spent thirty-three years trying to do the best I can at balancing each role. At moments I failed miserably and at other times I've succeeded by God's grace. Balancing is a continual process. It requires lots of sorting priorities and making choices every day.

Here are some areas that need to stay in balance. Examining them can help us make good choices as we face the challenges of each new day.

- Are you an Anti-Stuff-Person or a Stuff-Person?

    An Anti-Stuff-Person says if something is still serviceable, I don't need another. An Anti-Stuff-Person needs to balance by updating clothes and personal items because a good witness should look good.

    A Stuff-Person says more is better and newer is nicer. Stuffers can overdo purchases. There's nothing wrong with liking and wanting stuff unless it becomes a consuming focus or the "stuff" requires an excessive amount of your time and attention. Then it throws you off balance. That's probably why Colossians 3:1–2 reads: "You have been raised to life with Christ, so set your hearts on the things that are in heaven, where Christ sits on His throne at the right side of the Father. Keep your mind fixed there not on things on earth" (TEV).

- Are you a social person or an introvert?

    If you tend to be an introvert, you need to spend some time around people. It's God's design that His people show love for one another. On the other hand, if you're highly social, it's easy to be on the run constantly which can detract from your rest as well as your work. You need to find time alone with God.

- Do you love change or resist change?

Whatever your feelings about it, change will come. Life is like a kaleidoscope of constantly moving pictures and colors, and whenever a circumstance in your life changes—you get a new boss, your children start a new school year, your children are off for the summer, your father needs extra care, you move—you need to rebalance. All these situations create change and require decisions about the use of your time and energy.

On the other hand, too much change coming too quickly can be unsettling. Psychological stress tests always evaluate the number of recent changes in your life. Given a choice, make major changes slowly or keep them to a minimum.

Find your place of peace and balance in the Lord by spending time with Him. Then you can enjoy life whatever goes on around you.

Myra had trouble balancing herself. She asked God, "Show me where to focus my energy and my time, Lord. In every area where I have a choice, guide me into Your best for me at the moment."

Before taking on something extra, Myra learned to first evaluate her present responsibilities. She checked if she was having enough quiet time with God, then if she was meeting the needs of her husband and family. Only if Myra was sure she would not be neglecting these highest responsibilities did she add some other activity to her life.

God taught me this lesson about balancing my priorities through the illness of our son. Before he became sick I was very involved in college teaching and completing my doctoral degree. I thought what I was doing was extremely important and rewarding. Then I found I needed to eliminate almost all my activities in order to have time to meet my son's needs during his frequent hospitalizations and treatments. I never even missed my former activities—and I wasn't as indispensable as I thought! My former responsibilities continued fine with my replacements taking over.

Exploring Scripture

The book of Proverbs contains great practical instruction for balancing the priorities and activities of your life. There are thirty-one chapters. You might try reading one chapter each day to correspond with the day of the month. For example you would read chapter 9 on the ninth of every month. Highlight every Proverb that applies directly to you that day. Proverbs covers all the areas where you need to stay in balance, areas such as:

- self-righteousness versus hatred of evil
- wisdom versus foolishness
- generosity versus stinginess
- laziness versus diligence.
- order versus chaos

When God touches your life, He gives you a craving for balance and an unrest when you tilt too far off balance. If you let him, He'll reorder all your priorities.

Taking Action

- What tends to throw you out of kilter?

- When you know you're off-balance, how do you get realigned?

Lord, Your Word is clear. Time with You is my first priority, and time with my family is my second priority. May I weigh the importance of every other commitment in the light of Your Word and daily walk a steady and balanced path.

THIRTY–SIX

Being Christ's Body

*J*oan works two jobs, keeps her home immaculate, and enjoys close contact with her two adult sons. She takes "being Christ" to the people in her life seriously and ministers to the women she works with through notes, birthday parties for single parents, and outings planned for them. She and her husband have loaned furniture and helped with child care and household moves. They welcome houseguests frequently, even entertaining the parents of their friends. Joan has had recurring health problems, but instead of feeling sorry for herself, she's continued to care for others.

Is Joan overly energetic? She doesn't appear to be, nor does she ever seem to be in a hurry. She has simply found ways to use her talents for others in need. Not many of us could keep up with Joan, but there are ways to be helpful that anyone with a willing heart can do.

The first and most powerful thing you can do for a friend going through a difficult time is to pray for that person daily. Then make the call, stop by—that's the hardest. Forget about this "I don't want to intrude" falsehood that permeates modern society. If your friend wants to be left alone, your friend can tell you. Even if that's true, your friend will still be glad you offered to be present and available to her. During an intense crisis, don't let more than a few days go by without contacting your friend. During a long-term problem, don't let more than a week or two go by.

Encourage your friend to continue in his or her typical schedule. It's easy to drift into a feeling of hopelessness and despair when going through a tough time. Following a normal routine in waking and sleeping and other activities is important—perhaps most beneficial when a person doesn't feel like doing it.

Let your talk focus on the real concerns of your friend who's going through crisis. Don't become unnerved and shy away from discussing your friend's painful situation. If you have been through a similar problem, don't hesitate to share pointers you learned, especially biblical principles that apply to the situation and aided you. Often God puts a person into your life because you're in an excellent position to help.

Be honest. If you're worried about someone or see them choosing harmful activities—sleeping too much, ignoring their problem—say, "I'm concerned about . . ."

Be dependable. If you say you'll do something for a person, whatever it is—a visit, a errand, a phone call—do it. This isn't a time when a person can handle even small disappointments easily.

Help your friend make well-considered personal decisions. Feelings of fear and insecurity can entice a person to grab at any solution offered.

If listening to your friend isn't enough or the issue is very complex, by all means encourage your friend to speak to a pastor or counselor. As you listen to your friend's concerns, never downplay the dilemma or your friend's feelings about it. It's insulting to them if you try to minimize what they're going through even if the situation would not be as difficult for you.

Offer practical day-to-day help with your friend's responsibilities, but don't make arrangements without asking first if it's OK. A person going through a crisis already feels helpless and needs to get a sense of control over life.

Your friend may neglect her appearance at this time. Take her shopping, ask if you may accompany her for a haircut, try to help whatever the need may be. This kind of concern can lift someone's spirit immeasurably.

Don't expect anything in return. When you have a need, your friend may not even be sensitive enough to see it. Perhaps your friend's own emotions are still too raw from her problem. Pray to God and let Him choose whom He will send to minister to you.

Now, here are *three warnings:*

1. Watch out for Satan's twisting attacks on your service as you act as the body of Christ to others. Helping out at a homeless shelter or food pantry is wonderful, but not at the expense of personal time with Christ or personal outreach.

2. Do not be critical of women or men who do not choose to participate in the Christian service you think they are equipped to do. Within the church as well as without, be ready to praise and compliment others. Stay away from the strife-mongers. Either your words or your critical spirit will ultimately make its way back to those who you criticized. I know of several instances of grown sons and daughters who no longer attend church because they saw the pain their parents experienced over unkind words from other church members.

   As you focus fully on knowing Christ more, meeting your family responsibilities, and being Christ's body to others, you won't have time to judge anyone else.

3. Many of these acts of kindness will require time away from your family. Your family always comes first. Their needs must not be neglected while you minister to others. Otherwise your own family may develop a spirit of bitterness.

Often a person in need will enjoy a brief visit to your home and can spend time there. Your time of caring for others will develop a greater spirit of helpfulness and compassion in your husband and children as long as you don't overdo your service beyond what is pleasing to God (yes, this can happen).

Exploring Scripture

First Corinthians 12:13–14 says, "For by one Spirit we were all baptized into one body—whether Jews or Greeks, whether slaves or free—and have all been made to drink into one Spirit. [We could add whether we be rich or poor, brown, black or white, attractive or unattractive.] For in fact the body is not one member but many."

• What is the scriptural basis for our connection with others?

"Therefore, as the elect of God, holy and beloved, put on tender mercies, kindness, humility, meekness, longsuffering; But above all these things put on love, which is the bond of perfection. And let the peace of God rule in your hearts, to the which also you were called in one body; and be thankful" (Col. 3:12, 14–15).

• What qualities of spiritual life am I demonstrating to others in Christ's body?

✎ Taking Action

- Relate a time when a friend helped you go through a crisis. What help did you find most comforting?

- Which of the helps listed above do you feel most comfortable providing for others?

- What do you need to do for someone in need right now that you're neglecting?

Heavenly Father, within Your family are many who need love and care. You know those who need the attention I can give and I want to be available. Open my eyes to see these needs and respond as You would have me.

ঙ্ক THIRTY–SEVEN ৶

Aging with Grace

*E*ver wonder what life will be like when your youthful looks are gone? Or perhaps you are already in the class called "senior." Back in high school and college being a "senior" was viewed as a good thing. But all of a sudden regarding age "senior" has lost its status as advanced or better, and it's often the source of jokes and put-downs. We can't change the attitude of our culture toward aging, but we can change our own attitudes.

My mother, who is almost eighty, doesn't want to be called a "senior citizen." She is like many people for whom the idea of growing old seems scary. New kinds of insecurities, like fear of poor health and concern about sufficient finances, often pop up.

But the five basic psychological needs remain the same at any age. We all need

- To be in a relationship based on love.

  Without a special regard from someone, any of us can develop social hostility. Jenna wasn't receiving love because of the death of her family, so she gave love and did good for people around her who did not deserve or expect it. Soon they began to reciprocate and love her.

- To maintain a measure of security.

  An understanding of the life, death, and resurrection of Jesus is the greatest security we can have, for none of us can ever experience complete security in this life.

- To find an opportunity for ongoing creative expression(s) in our work or our home.

  Ann moved to a condo and left the gardening she loved because her husband was tired of keeping up with the grass and his pride wouldn't let him hire a yard service. Ann developed severe arthritis and seldom left her bed because she had lost her favorite creative outlet.

- To be appreciated by someone.

  Mary, a seventy-year-old capable waitress, quit her job where she felt loved by her customers and retired with her husband to Arkansas. She died within the year.

- To stay actively involved in life.

  Simple things like a trip to the store or a fun conversation with an interesting person can brighten up our lives. Kay moved in with her children and spent her days home alone while they were at work. She didn't drive and never reached out for friends through senior citizen groups. She became nervous, fearful, and forgetful. Don't live a minute of your life in fear of death.

Ellen, a "senior" client of mine, has had three facelifts. But they haven't lasted. She hates the idea of growing old. Why do some women spend half their lives trying to hide the fact that they're getting older? Aging is natural, inevitable, and irreversible. Older women are beautiful like the shine of soft chintz that's been enjoyed in the process of living.

What advice did I give to Ellen who's so concerned about aging? I suggested, "Keep your hair nicely styled and your grooming as careful as ever. But most important of all, keep your life purposeful. Stay focused spiritually. God the Father, Son, and Holy Spirit are the source of your vitality.

"Stay in charge of your life as much as you can even if you are in an assisted-living environment. Whenever you lose old friends because they move away or die, seek a new friendship to fill the void. Remember that emotions vary, but peace in the Lord is consistent.

"Don't become critical of the world because the pace is too fast or blame the young because they are too busy to visit you. Explore recent changes in the culture, like technology, with an open mind. Look for activities you can enjoy at a pace that's pleasant for you.

"Continue to use your gifts. I have read accounts of people diagnosed with degenerative diseases and senility who had amazing 'cures' when they got involved in exciting new activities. If you truly can't get around well, you can still have a powerful prayer ministry. Pray for God to show you ministries as well as individuals who need your daily prayers.

"Avoid dawdling, move purposefully. Never stop exercising, never stop eating well. You are always God's temple. Rest more if you need to, but do spend some time each day with other people, including children. It will keep you feeling vitally involved in this mutual adventure called life. When it's time to move into eternity, welcome the new adventure."

 *Exploring Scripture*

Psalm 103:5 says, "Who satisfies your mouth with good things, so that your youth is renewed like the eagle's."

- What does God do for His people all throughout our lives?

In Hebrews 3:14 we read, "For we continue to share in all that Christ has for us so long as we steadily maintain until the end the trust with which we began" (PHILLIPS).

- What is Christ's promise to us as we near the end of our lives? What are we to maintain until the end?

Remember the promises of God: God's Word says He will give us the desires of our hearts (Psalm 37:4). He doesn't add until we're fifty or sixty or eighty-five. Our job is to stay tuned in to the Holy Spirit and find out what those desires should be and then live in joyful expectation of seeing God work no matter how old we are.

Taking Action

Whatever age you are, remember if you want to have a cheerful, kindly disposition in old age, you need to work on developing those traits now. The major problem older people have is not their physical limitations but the psychological limitations they create for themselves by poor thought control.

- Which of the tips for aging with grace do I need to incorporate into my own life?

- Think of a recent situation where you reacted with grumbling, crabbiness, or worry. Describe how the same situation could have been handled with acceptance, determination, and cheerfulness.

Dear Lord, we are all on the same path—time is passing. I want every moment of this precious life You have given me to count by Your standards. Keep me going, Lord, and keep me looking forward to each step of the way, knowing heaven and eternity with You are always my goal.

Resolving Conflicts

I always include conflict resolution skills as part of marriage and family counseling. Conflict resolution is not a power struggle where one side wins, but is a method for solving disagreements so that both sides are pleased with the outcome.

Kerry caused great damage to her husband's self-esteem and their marital relationship by refusing to listen to her husband when she didn't agree with him. She had never really attempted to work through their differences in a calm, loving manner; instead, anytime a serious problem arose she threatened divorce. One day her husband shocked her by responding, "Go ahead, I don't care any more."

Conflicts will arise anytime two or more people try to get along—especially in a close relationship; conflicts are a natural part of life. But there are healthy and unhealthy ways to deal with these conflicts, and continually threatening divorce as Kerry did is not the healthy way. Before any of us start to try to resolve a conflict, we need to pray for God to bring us to a mutually agreeable resolution. Then we need to follow these guidelines:

1. Resolve a conflict quickly. (But if you sense that you're too upset or your temper is totally out of control, wait a little while!) Schedule a time when you can sit down to talk though the issue and resolve it. A disagreement can be like a rolling snowball. It keeps on growing until you stop it.

2. Before expressing a complaint, always express your genuine appreciation about another behavior of your husband or child. Avoid using derogatory phrases like "That was a dumb thing to do."

3. Use specific, clear words that describe the behavior you didn't like.

4. Restate what your partner or child says to make sure you understand the other point of view. Don't just assume you know how the other person is thinking or feeling—ask them.

5. Stay on one issue at a time. Don't get sidetracked. Especially be careful to avoid throwing in past behaviors that have been forgiven.

6. Brainstorm together for how this might have been handled differently.

7. Eliminate words like "You never" or "You always" or "I can't" or "I'll never be able to" or "You should" or "You shouldn't." They divide rather than unite.

8. If the other person won't listen or tends to yell, try passing an object back and forth. Try a spoon if you're in a restaurant or a golf ball at home. The person holding the object speaks, then passes the object to the other person. This provides each person an opportunity to speak calmly without being interrupted. It's a simple but effective listening technique. Another suggestion is to try writing a letter; use word pictures like "I feel like a plant that never gets watered."

9. Leave other relatives' traits and personality issues out of the discussion. If the person you're dealing with doesn't stick to the immediate conflict, make sure you do anyway.

10. If after you've both had your say and you're no closer to a resolution, pray together (or silently if the other person refuses). Wait for God to work. Do whatever He suggests. Sometimes His answer may be to keep still.

Exploring Scripture

Read Matthew 26:31–35. How did Jesus handle disagreements? Over and over in the Gospels we read that He patiently sat down and told His disciples they had drawn the wrong conclusion and explained what they needed to do. Jesus had conflicts with Peter. Jesus told Peter, "Peter, you are going to deny me when I'm arrested and you're confused about what to do next." Peter said, "I won't deny my ties with you; I'll be loyal." But Jesus knew better. After the Resurrection, He gently reminded Peter. Finally Peter got the idea. Jesus didn't give up on Peter; He forgave Peter when he didn't measure up. He gave Peter lots of chances.

That's what you and I need too—lots of chances. We all do, and we need to give them to others as well.

Taking Action

Set a cassette player to record yourself the next time you want to discuss something your husband or child is doing that you don't like. Evaluate how you handled the situation in light of the conflict resolution guidelines above.

- Did I express genuine appreciation? What positive things did I say?

- Did I allow the other person to explain their side of the issue, and did I listen?

Keep these resolution guidelines on the side of the refrigerator or posted in a cabinet where you can reread them from time to time.

Lord, I want to get along with the people I love in a healthy way, facing honestly any problems between us and taking care of them as quickly and kindly as possible. At these times I need the patience and courage and wisdom that only comes from the Holy Spirit.

Breaking Negative Patterns

*O*ften clients come into my office who have been struggling in some area and over a period of time have developed negative habits to deal with their struggles. They now realize that these thought patterns or behaviors are unpleasant, annoying, and possibly sinful, but they feel powerless to stop them.

Here are some typical negative patterns. Sue is in bondage to procrastination and disorder. Jane has a compulsive need to have *perfect* order in her home. She gets depressed over any mess and yells at her children constantly. Ann always looks picture-perfect when she goes somewhere and gets compliments on her appearance, but she leaves her home looking like it's been burglarized. Karen's in bondage as a never-say-no do-gooder. She gets pats on the back for being so helpful which cover her negative patterns of low self-esteem and a sense of purposeless.

For some women a negative pattern might be the tendency to gossip about others by disguising it as "sharing prayer concerns." As they pray, instead of feeling compassion, they may feel a tinge of superiority that they don't have this problem.

A negative pattern can become a major spiritual struggle if it's allowed to spread. It's like when I got poison oak. First the rash was minor and contained on one area of my skin. The next thing I knew it had entered my bloodstream and began to spread throughout my body. The itching became torture. No topical ointment helped until I recognized what I had and treated the deeper infection within my blood with steroids and antihistamines.

I often find explanations for women's present responses and negative patterns in their past experiences. Sometimes a parent never expressed love for them, or there was too much pressure to excel coupled with lack of success in school. But explanations alone aren't enough to solve the problem. Once individuals admit their negative patterns, they must avoid fixating on the reasons for them ad nauseam over months or years.

Understanding causes alone doesn't change negative thoughts and behaviors.

Clients need to decide both that they want to be free from these patterns and that they need God's help to be set free from destructive habits that hold them in bondage and keep them from living as God intended. That's the treatment part. Entire books have been written on the subject of right thinking, but there's not enough power in positive thinking or intellectual knowledge to be set free. The power comes from God.

The main principles needed to set us free from any bondage or negative pattern in our lives come straight from God's Word. If you've been clinging to a destructive pattern, these steps can help you change successfully:

- Ask God to help you pattern your habits after those of Jesus.

    Study His Word to learn how you ought to think and act. Then put into practice the truths you read; it's not enough to pray and then wait for God to change you! God has given you the responsibility to respond to His Word with your actions.

- Name any negative pattern(s) you recognize in yourself.

    If you can identify the reason you've been drawn into this negative pattern, write that down too, or ask a friend whose confidentiality you can trust to help you find the source of the bondage.

- Replace a negative pattern with a positive pattern as soon as you are aware of it.

    For example, replace impatience with compassion. You are changed by "renewing your mind"—you can't simply remove a negative attitude or behavior by suppressing it.

- Desensitize yourself, little by little, by thinking and acting the opposite of your former way.

    Choose to think and act as if you have this habit under control. That's what Paul calls "setting your mind" in Colossians 3. Paul also talks about "putting to death" (these old patterns won't die on their own, you need to kill them), "ridding yourselves," and "putting on" the good and the positive. Yes, act that way, even if only briefly at first, until the new thoughts and behaviors become natural.

 *Exploring Scripture*

Study and memorize Psalm 16:5–11 (NIV) to break negative thought patterns and fix your mind on the good patterns God has promised you. With all this good going for you, why stay stuck in negatives?

> LORD, you have assigned me my portion and my cup;
>> you have made my lot secure.
> The boundary lines have fallen for me in pleasant places;
>> surely I have a delightful inheritance.
> I will praise the LORD, who counsels me,
>> Even at night my heart instructs me.
> I have set the LORD always before me.
>> Because He is at my right hand,
>> I will not be shaken.
> Therefore my heart is glad and my tongue rejoices,
>> my body also will rest secure,
>> because you will not abandon me to the grave,
>> nor will you let your Holy One see decay.
> You have made known to me the path of life;
>> you will fill me with joy in your presence,
>> with eternal pleasures at your right hand.

If you're tempted to doubt that change is possible, meditate on 2 Corinthians 5:17. "If anyone is in Christ, he is a new creation, old things have passed away; behold, all things have become new."

For further application memorize Phillipians 4:8.

Taking Action

- What negative patterns do I allow to control my life?

- Write a description of the positive thought pattern or behavior you will develop in place of a negative one. Ask a prayer partner to pray daily for you to find a positive replacement for this negative pattern.

Lord, I hate some of the things I do even while I'm doing them. Give me both the patience to practice new behaviors and the will to keep at it so that I will be daily transformed into Your image.

‿৯ও FORTY ৫৵‿

Encouraging Communication

*W*ould you like to have a guest in your home who never stopped talking and insisted on all your husband's and children's attention? And to top it off—the guest taught your children behavior that you didn't want them to learn! How long would that person be welcome? Well, if there's a TV in your home, you already have this type of guest!

Lorie wanted to improve communication in her family, and she knew TV viewing was preventing frequent normal family conversation. Lorie knew she needed to limit TV time in her home.

One of the greatest blocks to a healthy relationship between children and parents is television. Children immersed in television simply don't know how to find pleasure in everyday talk. The same thing can happen if your child or husband spends a lot of time on the computer. TVs and computers are similar to an addictive drug. They suck the watcher insidiously into a dependence so that when the screen is off, the person feels uncomfortable and like something is missing. An extended deprivation of a couple days causes irritability and moodiness.

Not only does TV promote violence, which you've heard repeatedly (and not enough has been done to eliminate it), but TV actually harms children. I see it in children I counsel. TV can make children passive communicators. These children will respond when adults ask them direct questions, but they don't initiate questions and conversation. In effect they lose the ability to communicate spontaneously and act bored and sullen in response to the life around them; they become uninvolved in normal activities.

Many families have removed the TV completely. I'm not totally against TV, but I am opposed to its taking over as the most powerful "family communicator." I suggest one hour a night maximum is a good rule, except possibly for a sports or outdoors program which models activity and seems to encourage activity. I'm in favor of controlled TV. One hour means an occasional show or two.

I've had moms tell me, "TV is so wonderful when my kids are sick." Up to a point, that's true. But remember how, as children, many of us enjoyed the extra attention we received from a parent during illness— being fussed over, playing games, or being read to. Isn't that better?

I'm not as much *against* the TV/computer as I'm *for* family communication and fun. Establishing good family communication requires attentive planning—it doesn't just happen! If you've already taken steps to reduce or eliminate TV viewing, what alternative activities are you providing? Remember it's important to replace a negative pattern with a positive. You may not be able to withstand your children's moans otherwise. Withdrawal takes at least six weeks to two months, and you need to be prepared.

Here are some tips for encouraging family communication:

1. Don't expect strong relationships to simply happen. Take the responsibility for improving your relationship with God, your husband, your children, and the other significant people in your life.
2. Think ahead of conversational starters for family dinnertimes just as you would with adult friends.
3. Take time to play *with* your children and not simply plan fun activities for them. Keep badminton set up in the yard and swing a racket around after dinner with your family, play board games, walk the dog together.
4. Ideally find some activities that each of your children enjoy and plan a time for sharing these activities with them.
5. Make silly talk occasionally.
6. Model and teach good listening skills. Slow down, make eye contact, practice listening for "feelings" as well as words.
7. Be especially sensitive to your younger children when an older brother or sister dominates family sharing time. Be alert to younger children's needs when an older child leaves the home for school or marriage. This can be a difficult adjustment period for the child(ren) still at home because the family dynamic changes. You may be experiencing a sense of loss as well, but you'll help yourself by focusing on your family's needs and planning fun times with your child(ren) at home.
8. Follow the "A Little" principle: "A little alone time, a little family time, a little planned time, a little unplanned time, a little TV, a little self-generated entertainment."

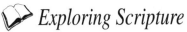 Exploring Scripture

What principles does God's Word give for TV and for family communication? The same as for playing tennis and washing your car. It says nothing specific, but there is a general principle worth noting. First Corinthians 14:40 says, "Let all things be done decently and in order." This great verse on order was originally applied to church meetings but is appropriate for every activity involving Christians.

- How does planning our family time decently and in order affect our use of the TV? Our planning of wholesome family activities?

Taking Action

- Which family communication activities listed above could be implemented first in your family?

- What two things can you do this week to promote opportunities for family communication?

꧁꧂

Heavenly Father, I do not want to take the "easy way out" in planning our family times. Guide me as I seek wholesome activities for us to do together. We want to share in special times that build a healthy future for all of us, and I need to take the time to plan and make these arrangements.

Equipping Children

*J*oanna came into my office to see how she could make her twenty-six-year-old daughter more independent. I asked, "Does your daughter have the skills she needs for independent living?" "No," she admitted. When Joanna's daughter and son were growing up, Joanna did everything for them. Her children became self-centered from her unhealthy focus on constantly pleasing them and dominating their lives by being involved in everything they did. Was she smothering or mothering her children? Merely babying or training them? Mothering and training are positive—smothering and babying aren't.

As a child Joanna had never had activities outside school because her parents both worked. She wanted her children to have these "opportunities" so she tended to say "yes" to everything. When she was growing up, Joanna hadn't had many friends. As a parent, she'd always said "yes" to anything her children wanted to do with other children because she wanted them to have lots of friends. As a result there was no time left for her children to help out at home, so Joanna did everything.

When her children became young adults, their demanding expectations continued, but Joanna no longer had the stamina or desire to keep the pace. I helped Joanna understand the source of her feelings and become secure enough to risk displeasing her adult children when she needed to nicely say, "Handle it yourself."

It would have helped immeasurably in their personal development if Joanna had taught her children the skills they needed to cope for themselves, starting with small household responsibilities. Moms, chores are wonderful! Teach children to enjoy them! And along the way every child needs to memorize Colossians 3:23, "Whatever you do, do it heartily, as to the Lord and not to men!"

We also need to train our children to use the proper methods to accomplish tasks. How often do we assign a task to our children and expect them to figure out how to do it? (And then we complain because it wasn't done right.) In 1 Chronicles 22:5–11, notice how David made the preparations and laid the groundwork for his son Solomon's success before he gave the command to Solomon to get to work building the temple. Then David prayed for the Lord to help make Solomon successful. He specifically told his son to be careful to observe all the laws of God in order to be successful. He encouraged Solomon to be strong and courageous—not afraid or discouraged. Solomon, David's son, had to do the work. David made sure Solomon was equipped, told him clearly what to do, and had other men available to help him.

Once children are grown, married, and have children, they need to be capable of living on their own (although occasionally they may need help *briefly*). But emotional and spiritual parenting is a lifelong process. Children don't ever outgrow their need for advisors and encouragers.

📖 *Exploring Scripture*

Every child needs to be told about the Lord. In Psalm 22:30 we read, "Posterity will serve him; future generations will be told about the LORD" (NIV).

Ephesians 6:2–3 is the first commandment with a promise attached, "Honor your father and mother . . . that it may go well with you and that you may enjoy long life on earth" (NIV). Prepare your children for success in this world by teaching them to honor the Lord as well as those in authority over them, starting with you.

✏️ *Taking Action*

Are you doing too much on a daily basis for your children? What tasks can you "hand off" to them right now? Have you trained your children as well in manners, social customs, and people skills as you have provided academics for them? When children are overly dependent on their home environment, they sometimes become overly dependent on the school environment when they go off to college (which is why they delay graduating).

- Where do I need to begin preparing my children to become more independent? What responsibilities can I give to them now?

- Am I equipping them to deal with life apart from academic skills? List ten practical things your children should be able to do as an older teen.

Lord, I love my children and I love helping them. Help me to discern the needed mothering from the unhealthy tendency to keep them dependent on me. Help me to continually build both their "roots" and their "wings."

Loving the First Corinthians 13 Way

I couldn't believe it; I really thought there must have been a misprint in Scripture when I first read in 1 Corinthians 13:5, "It [love] is not irritable or touchy" (LB). That means love does not take offense! There have been times I've wanted to yell, "Not take offense, but do you know what he or she did to ME? Surely this situation is different!" Wrong!

It's easiest to see the faults of and be offended by people that we're around often which is why marriage and other close relationships are a challenge for 1 Corinthians 13-style love.

Yet God expects love to be the norm for us Christians, and He specified the way to make that happen. He never asks us to do something without giving us the tools and equipment needed to get the task done. Loving *without taking offense* is the key in our continuing to love and continuing to keep our promises and our commitments.

I've often failed at that miserably. In the early days of my marriage, I used to make mental lists of my husband's offenses to tell a friend once a week. Instead of feeling better after I shared my "hurts," I simply fired up my anger. My husband would wonder why I'd come home so annoyed and tense after my evening out.

I knew there were lots of other young wives with attitudes similar to what mine had been. Anna was a lovely teenager I met soon after she became a Christian. I lost track of her until she turned twenty-eight and came to me for counseling. Although still very beautiful, Anna was now a nervous woman—her hands shook, her voice was a monotone. Her face had lost its serenity, and her eyes no longer held the glow of joy. What had happened to her?

After visiting with Anna a half hour, I identified her problem. It could be summed up in the words, "Love is not irritable or touchy" from

1 Corinthians 13. Anna had written her own mental book of all the offenses committed against her by her family, her friends, her church, and on and on. Some friends didn't call her enough; somebody else dropped in too often. Anna couldn't forgive her pastor for his insensitive comments to her husband although she said she'd tried over and over. What she really meant was "I *won't* forgive him." She considered attending another church because she could no longer get anything from the pastor's sermons. Anna explained to me how upset these people had become when she pointed out how they offended her.

"But aren't you supposed to tell people how you feel?" she asked. In intimate relationships, yes. And if people are committing sin, Scripture has a clear plan for addressing the problem. But if you just don't like something or are slightly inconvenienced, then, no. There's been too much "Let all your feelings hang out" in every area of life imaginable.

The saddest thing of all is that Anna had long ago lost her own joy and her peace by her habit of taking offense. Love must be slow to lose patience, and our model here is God's patience with us. Constructive patience and kindness includes positive words and not expecting or demanding apologies from others who have wronged us. It is God who makes all things right.

Certainly if a Christian is in sin, yes, the problem must be taken up with that individual. But if a person's behavior is simply annoying us, that's our opportunity to practice love and draw on God's grace. Often *deciding* not to get annoyed and *practicing* silence is the best answer. It's certainly better than Anna's solution.

So many wedding ceremonies include 1 Corinthians 13, the "Love Chapter," among their Scripture readings, yet few marriages or other relationships follow its guidelines for not taking offense. I certainly need to reread this chapter every day of my life and apply it as my sermon to live by.

As hard as our pastoral staff, our business associates, our family, or our friends try, we will be offended by what they do or don't do or say. But Jesus loves us, and we must love others. If you, too, struggle in this regard, hang this motto where you'll see it often: Love Every Offense Away. Not taking offense sounds hard, but it's for the tough areas like this that God generously pours out His great grace—or none of us would ever succeed!

Exploring Scripture

Read 1 Corinthians 13 aloud as if the words were spoken just for you. By far the hardest part of this chapter to live are verses 5 and 7 (NIV). "[Love] is not rude, it is not self-seeking, it is not easily angered, it keeps no record of wrongs." "It always protects, always trusts, always hopes, always perseveres" (vv. 5, 7 NIV). J. B. Phillips puts love this way: "Love has good manners and does not pursue selfish advantage. It is not touchy. It does not keep account of evil or gloat over the wickedness of other people."

Taking Action

- God loves me and forgives me the 1 Corinthians 13 way. How do I want to love and forgive others?

On a separate sheet of paper, make a list of all the people who have offended you or are offending you right now. Then tear up the paper and resolve not to dwell on how you've been hurt ever again! Only God's grace makes this difficult *act of the will* possible. I often do this exercise in counseling sessions between husbands and wives. One wife refused to destroy her list. She wanted to keep bringing the subject up again and again. She would not let go of her past hurts, and her counseling sessions proved ineffective.

Heavenly Father, my mind is full of lists of offenses and perceived wrongs and these lists are very precious to me. Parting with my list is like parting with a dear friend—but not a friend—an enemy that keeps Your love from flowing freely through me to others. By an act of my will I tear up my list and I choose to forgive.

⊰ FORTY–THREE ⊱

Hearing God

$\mathcal{K}$ara, a young career woman, said, "It's not that I have any doubt that God can speak to me, but I'm not important enough that He'd speak to me. Besides, how could I hear His words without distorting them?"

I responded, "Isn't that an insult to the communicative ability of God who wants to be understood? Don't you think He can make His message clear? Didn't He create you with a spiritual antenna to hear Him?"

Eventually Kara realized she had dulled her relationship with God with a meaningless routine of rote prayers. God's mercies are new every morning, but she wasn't experiencing them. She needed a reminder that His communication is always available and is a sign of His mercy and kindness.

The real difficulty in hearing God is a six-letter word, L-I-S-T-E-N. I took a survey of how many people spend five minutes a day listening to God, and my survey found that listening is probably the most neglected act of piety.

My husband and I had hectic schedules for several weeks. We were running in different directions, and I could sense myself drawing apart from him—not divulging my intimate thoughts because he wasn't available. At one point I thought sadly, "Wayne is missing out on some insights I'd like to share about the children and other matters, and I'm missing hearing the special moments of his days." We both had other priorities that seemed more pressing than our need for time together.

God reminded me that that's how He feels when I don't schedule time for Him. I start to feel distant from God and don't express my intimate prayer thoughts and needs. I can't hear His voice as well. Yet I know He hasn't broken our connection—I have. I miss out on the wisdom and guidance He wants to share with me.

God is in creative contact with us throughout the day. He can use other people and even nature to demonstrate His presence in our lives. How do I actually practice listening to God?

First comes setting aside the time, then what? The next requirement is putting my own thoughts aside—my ideas of what God should say to me. I need to be prepared for anything.

Here's the sort of thing I may hear: He may urge me to do something or He may want me to do nothing but praise Him. He may show me a principle for someone else I know and guide me to share it in love. He may give me a sense of His awesome love right now even in my human imperfection. (That's my favorite kind of communication.) He may lead me to a book or a portion of Scripture that speaks to a need in my life at the moment. He may guide me through a strong impression to a certain course of action. I have heard God in each of these ways at different times.*

 ## Exploring Scripture

Look up 1 Samuel 3:10, "Speak, for your servant hears." That was the response of Samuel and many other Scripture giants to God's voice.

- Can you name some people in Scripture whose lives were totally changed by what God revealed to them?

 ## Taking Action

- How much listening time do you give God each day, each week? Pretend Jesus is sitting in the front seat of the car when you run errands. Chat with Him. What is He saying to you? Go out for coffee and sit alone in a booth. Pretend He's across from you. Talk to Him in your heart. Read a Scripture passage and write down your impressions of what it means for your life right now. Whatever type of situation it takes for you to begin to hear God, do it until hearing Him is such a natural joy, you can't bear to miss it!

꧁꧂

Speak, Lord, I am listening. I am listening through Scripture; I am listening in my heart; I am listening through the voices of my friends and loved ones; I am listening through nature. I am listening for Your voice.

---

* To further hear God, read *God Calling* and *God at Eventide* by A. J. Russell (Barbour, 1950). These two books offer reassurance of God's personal love and guidance.

FORTY–FOUR

Entertaining God's Way

Two of our best friends, Tom and Pat, have brought more than a hundred people to Christ by inviting strangers they meet to dinner at their home. They have a modest home, and if Pat doesn't have time to clean and polish as she wants, Pat keeps the lights dim and burns a lot of candles.

Is this pleasing to God or what? If Jesus were walking through her town, Pat would be ready to say, "Stop over and spend the night." She could also easily say, "I'll have some friends in to meet you."

From His frequent contact with people, Jesus stressed the importance of spending time with others. After all, how can we love our neighbors if we're locked in our own houses each night staring at TV or isolated at home with our own families?

Luke 14 could be called the "party chapter" in Scripture. Read it aloud and notice how often a dinner party or a gathering of friends is mentioned. Jesus gives two guidelines in this chapter for us when we entertain.

1. *When* we give a luncheon or dinner party, watch that we don't just invite friends of the same social status. Invite those who cannot repay our hospitality.
2. *When* we're the one invited, be a humble guest.

From Jesus' use of the word *when*, it's obvious Jesus expects us to be entertaining regularly. His message is "get out and party." The old Girl Scout song is still a great ditty, "Make new friends, but keep the old, some are silver and the others gold" (author unknown).

In the days of Jesus a host first invited a group of guests, then gave a second invitation after everything was prepared. There was always room for one or a few more, but a group took effort. Now we aren't supposed to imitate exactly the customs of Jesus' day; obviously, our culture is different, but we can extract the essence of its lessons for today.

Each of us can examine our mind-set toward entertaining. Do you see yourself in any of these examples?

When Carla was a child, she used to hate family parties because she came from an alcoholic background. Every time guests were invited, Carla did all the preparation beforehand, all the serving during, and the clean-up afterwards which exhausted her. Then the evening would inevitably end in a screaming match between her parents. When Carla married, her husband liked to have his family over for dinner often, and he insisted that the meal have two meats, two vegetables, rolls, a couple jellos, an assortment of relishes, and several desserts. It never occurred to him to help.

After counseling, Carla said, "I'm now balancing my husband's wishes with what I can handle comfortably. I used to identify easily with Martha in Scripture. But when my husband began to help me out in the kitchen, he began to understood that we could make a pot of soup the day before, toss a salad, and then serve the meal with loaves of French bread. He truly began to understand that our dinner was not the only meal our guests would eat all week. This way they could enjoy more of us. Food they can get anywhere."

Little by little Carla has learned to stay calm and relaxed as she prepares for company, but she's filled with excitement. She keeps the meal simple and now enjoys her dinner parties as much as her guests do.

Many women prefer to entertain friends in restaurants because it's too hard to get their houses in order for entertaining or they don't think their decor is nice enough. At times the convenience of meeting in a restaurant is the only way busy people can get together, but pleasant as restaurant food can be, the ambiance of sharing of our personal lifestyle is lost in entertaining out.

What makes entertaining in our homes exhausting is letting our pride get tangled up with enjoying our guests. Entertaining is not show-off time. If we show-off, our friends will feel they have to show off back. All the fun and relaxation disappears. Don't get me wrong. I've been down that street in the early years of my marriage, and, whew, it's not worth the frazzled nerves and marathon productions I used to make of a simple thing like company for dinner. I'd want this dinner to be really special, memorable, the best party/holiday ever. Why? Who did I exalt by having everything "just so"? Do you fit anywhere in these examples?

Here's an easy way to entertain a group that I saw when I was waiting to check out at the grocery store in Wisconsin last weekend. I watched as a lady emptied her cart on the counter next to me. She pulled out bags of prepared salads (the kind that are prewashed and include a bag of dressing and croutons and "dump and serve" are the directions), then she lifted out presliced, prebuttered loaves of garlic bread, a couple jars of spaghetti sauce, and some spaghetti noodles.

She'd have to spend twenty minutes watching the noodles and sticking bread in the oven. I figured she easily could feed about twenty people for about twenty-five dollars. Yes, that's more money than if she made everything herself, but compared to a restaurant tab, it's not high. Obviously she wouldn't be impressing her guests with her gourmet cooking skills, but the point is she was having a group in and being hospitable.

You can be ready to entertain Jesus and His disciples or your family and friends at any moment, too!

📖 *Exploring Scripture*

Read the story of Martha and Mary's entertaining. Don't you feel sorry for Martha with all that work to do and Mary wasn't helping, even though Jesus said Mary chose the best part? Didn't Jesus realize how tough it is to feed a crowd? Before you answer, read Luke 10:40, "Martha was *cumbered* about much serving" (KJV). "Cumber"—what an interesting word—it sounds so heavy and laborious, and that's what it meant. Phillips' translation reads, "But Martha was worried about her elaborate preparations."

What was Martha's problem? Jesus knew very well that Martha had "overcare in service." Martha needed to be corrected. She had become "cumbered" with her entertaining.

✏️ *Taking Action*

- Make a list of the people you'd like to entertain in the next several months.

Set a couple dinner dates for the next several weeks. Plan a basic, simple menu for dinner. Write the menu on a 3x5 card along with a shopping list on the back. Do all household projects and heavy cleaning the week before. Ask your children for special household help if you need it. Try to have everything done at least an hour before the guests are due. Walk through the rooms where your guests will be and pray they'll be blessed by their time in your home.

Prayerfully invite Jesus in advance to every party you have. Prepare some spiritual food to serve along with every meal. As you set the table, pray for your guests to be blessed by being in your home. Check *Reader's Digest* or *Guideposts* for some short inspirational stories you can share. Or talk about a current event and its moral implications. As the conversation lulls or as a related subject comes up, share the inspirational thoughts you've prepared.

Have fun! Jesus did and He wants you to also.

A note for further application in your family: Your family needs to be entertained as specially as guests occasionally. Dine in a place in your house where you don't usually eat. Set up a card table in the living room and serve dinner there. How about eating on the porch? Amazing how a change of scene slows children down. Prepare some family-sharing questions like: What would you like to do that you've never done before? What do you like most about each person here? Set the table extra special, maybe use placecards of poetry or Scripture verses for the children's names and let them guess which verse is theirs.

My home is open, Lord, to fill with the people You want to be there. Thank You for all the easy ways available today for me to get ready to serve my guests. Help me to think clearly and creatively as I prepare; keep me calm; keep my eyes on being a blessing and not on creating a masterpiece.

Staying Culturally Involved

I come from the generation I call the "Cross-over Women." I watched my mom run clothes through a wringer washer before the Maytag came into the basement, but I also read the *Feminine Mystique* by Betty Friedan the summer of my marriage. I was a yo-yo woman, alternating between fierce feminism and wishy-washy femininity until I met the living God and experienced the love of Jesus Christ.

The social culture and political culture are continually in a state of change—and we need to adjust to it, up to a point. Whenever our absolute Christian values or the values of Christians around us get confused in the bombardment of the world's philosophies, we need to be wise and vocal about speaking out and taking action with gentleness and courage.

That means if we're to help others successfully, we must stay involved with the world about us and not withdraw from it. For example, as a brand-new Christian, I seriously considered aborting our fourth child. I had a life-threatening problem with my third pregnancy which could have easily recurred. On top of that, my husband and I had a major blood incompatibility problem and had been advised not to have more children. The baby was expected to require a total blood transfusion at birth, which was a great risk. My big concern was who would raise our three other children if I died.

I had to decide what I believed about God's will and the purpose for every life. I was full of the cultural teaching around me, and abortion seemed like a logical choice. Several Christian people entered my life at this time. They had studied both sides of the issue and listened to my concerns. Without condemning me for considering abortion and without denying that it was the "world's" valid option, these friends helped me sort through my priorities in light of God's truth.

I decided to trust God and have the baby, even if it meant dying or caring for a handicapped child. During this time, many of my deep theological questions were resolved. Our son Daniel was delivered by cesarean section and neither of us had complications, praise God! I'm not proud to admit that abortion was a close call. The knowledge of both sides of the abortion issue that these intelligent, caring Christians presented to us helped us make the right decision. If they'd just preached at me, I know I would have been turned off. Of course God's forgiveness is always available to women, non-Christian and Christian, who chose abortion and questioned it later, and it's critically important for women to seek help and counseling in working through this experience.

Abortion is just one of many social and political issues needing our vigilance. Christian women must be vigilant in guarding against abuses of personal freedom.

Women need to be alert regarding the financial aid that the United States sends to countries that criticize us, and we must be alert regarding where we send American soldiers to risk their lives. Women need to keep the public schools teaching the basics and leaving the social issues to families. The entertainment industry needs vigilant women to guard against the slop it produces. We women must track local decision-making over events that concern our community, our city, and our schools.

Many Christian women aren't aware of the rights they have in the public domain. There are several Christian legal organizations like the American Center for Law and Justice (1000 Regent University Dr., Virginia Beach, Virginia), waiting to help people who are being persecuted on religious grounds.

Jim Russell established the Amy Foundation (3798 Capital City Blvd., Lansing, Michigan 48906), and he encourages every Christian church to become involved in the Christian Writer's Group Movement. Members meet regularly to write letters on local, state, and national issues that impact morality and Christian family life. Members of the group read, watch, and listen to the news regularly and then write editorials and articles. "Letters to the Editor" are widely read in most newspapers and are a valuable resource for Christian women to express their views. Jim Russell and his wife, Phyllis, use these guidelines:

1. Identify an issue in the news
2. Define the issue for the reader who may not have seen the original story
3. Apply biblical truth to the issue
4. Reinforce it with a quote from Scripture
5. Close with love

 *Exploring Scripture*

Read the book of Esther. Any confusion about whether or not to be involved actively in the culture around you should end when you study the gentle but firm Esther who developed both her wisdom and her feminine attractiveness. She used tact and careful planning in approaching the government of her day.

Read about the activist Priscilla who, together with her husband, Aquila, risked social pressure to support the apostles of Jesus. Acts 18:26 says, "So he [Apollos] began to speak boldly in the synagogue. When Aquila and Priscilla heard him, they took him aside and explained to him the way of God more accurately." Although they'd only recently come from Italy (Acts 18:1–3), Priscilla and Aquila started a church in their home (1 Corinthians 16:19).

Taking Action

Stay alert. Read the papers or a weekly news magazine. Listen to some talk radio. Understand BOTH sides of issues, but don't just read and listen. Do something! One call or letter every other week can become twenty-six a year. Keep a notepad in the kitchen and politely cover two areas when you call or write: first describe what you appreciated and would like continued or expanded, and then second, describe what concerns you and what you'd like done.

Call the library and ask the reference librarian or phone company to find the address you need to send the letter. As you accumulate a collection of addresses of TV stations, radio shows, and members of Congress, tape them inside a kitchen cabinet and share them with other women. Have your older children write letters too—a quick after-dinner family activity you can supervise along with clean-up. It builds good habits in your children, and children's letters are noticed.

Gather women together to watch and pray with you. Visit your movie theater, your school board, your local bookshop. Say pleasantly and firmly what your expectations are. Become an advocate for short-distance, personalized government. And be patient. Don't expect quick results, and don't quit!

❧

Lord, forgive me of the sin of standing by and letting others do the job of speaking up in our town, in our schools, and in our country. Keep me alert about current events and willing to make my voice heard in calls and letters. And keep me sensitive to ministry to my friends and acquaintances who may simply need an informed word from me to keep them from making a painful mistake.

Enduring Tests and Trials

No one likes to hear this, but Scripture tells us that there are times when God either allows or sends afflictions for the ultimate benefit of His children.

We all think it's great when we don't have to strain to meet challenges in life, when we can enjoy those blissful periods when there are no major relational flare-ups, no difficult job or school problems, when everyone in the family is healthy and happy! Maybe finances aren't abundant, but they're adequate for present needs. Then suddenly something goes wrong, and the sweet period comes to a halt. It's time to regroup and figure out how to survive the trials that have popped into our lives.

Sometimes these tests and trials come from Satan. Remember Ezra, the man who committed to serving God with his whole life? He was involved in rebuilding the temple of the Lord—a good thing, to be sure. In Ezra 4:4 we read, "Then the peoples around them set out to discourage the people of Judah and make them afraid to go on building. They hired counselors to work against them and frustrate their plans during the entire reign of Cyrus king of Persia and down to the reign of Darius king of Persia" (NIV). Ezra had to endure trials that came from his peers and people hired to thwart him.

God also sends trials Himself to accomplish His purposes in our lives. Some Christians don't like this idea, but if we deny a God who tests His people, we twist God's character to make Him into our image of how we'd like God to act.

Remember Abraham and Isaac in Genesis 22? Talk about a test of obedience—lay your son on the altar and offer him as sacrifice. But by then Abraham had learned that he could trust God—no matter what! And remember it was the Holy Spirit who urged Jesus to go into the desert to be tempted by the Devil. Yes, God *knew* Satan would test Jesus there! God uses all things, even tests and trials, for our good.

A fifty-year-old client of mine, Sally, was experiencing a difficult time. When her husband lost his career-track job, his ego drooped dangerously low. He was moody and depressed and began to speak belligerently to Sally and the children. He refused to get a low-paying job saying something great would turn up any day. Sally had put up with his attitude several months, but now she was getting fed up with it. Sally came to see me prepared to offer Frank an ultimatum: get any job and stop making everyone miserable. Both Sally and Frank were scared about the future. Frank still needed time to deal emotionally with his job loss.

Certainly change was in order. Not for a minute would I suggest that Sally shouldn't strive to help Frank improve his behavior, but the harshness of her demands could have pushed him to seek divorce papers. When I suggested God might be testing Sally's ability to show compassion and build her husband's esteem, Sally shook her head in disbelief. She was a woman of prayer who loved Jesus more than anything in life, but she couldn't believe that God would ever send her and her husband this trial.

Like many tenderhearted women, Sally wanted God to be an indulgent parent who protected her from any pain. Sally became angry with me when I pointed out that God sometimes sends trials to test or mature us. When this trial came, Sally preferred to blame it on Satan or the sinful nature of men and women. But there's nothing like testing to show a person's level of obedience and commitment.

Whatever the source of our trials today, God gives sufficient grace and strength to get through. We can expect trials in this life, but we can refuse to be overwhelmed by them. God is teaching and training us.

📖 Exploring Scripture

According to Psalm 119:71, "It was good for me to be afflicted so that I might learn your decrees" (NIV), and James 1:2, "My brethren, count it all joy when you fall into various trials, knowing that the testing of your faith produces patience," what benefits can come from affliction?

Read Jeremiah 35:1–19 to find out about the Recabites, some interesting people God tested. In this passage God told His prophet Jeremiah to give wine to the Recabites to drink despite the fact that they had a commitment to the founder of their religious order not to drink. The Recabites refused the wine. The Lord told Jeremiah to go to the men of Judah and compare the faithfulness of the Recabites to a human order with the Israelites' disobedience to the far more important commands of God. How did this test give God's people a powerful example?

 *Taking Action*

When our son developed cancer and we were praying for his healing, he was hit by a drunk driver and his leg was shattered. In looking back I believe Satan may have been trying to destroy our confidence in God, and God may have been testing our commitment to maintain our faith in Him when He allowed the second calamity.

- Describe a time when you feel God may have been testing your faith through a trial.

- Help your children endure affliction and God's testing in their lives by telling them how you've benefited from some of the trials of your past.

Lord, I long to grow and mature through the difficult times of my life. I long to experience them in the light of Your overall purposes for me, learning what I need to learn and being strengthened further for service.

❧ FORTY-SEVEN ❧

Training Children

I asked an experienced teacher at a local Christian school what parents should work on, and she answered, "They should discipline their children better. I have to train so many children to behave in school. Then the parents are amazed when I tell them how well their child responds to my rules, because the child's a terror at home."

Parents need to set consistent standards for their children and then firmly follow-through on those standards every day. Now many moms and dads do a great job with their kids, but often I see children being rushed into cars, dragged through grocery stores, ignored or yelled at one minute, and then being mindlessly pampered with promises and treats the next minute. One minute the children are marionettes and their parents are pulling the strings; the next minute they switch and the children pull the strings. I want to yell, "Stop! Think about what you're doing right now with this child. What are you teaching?" Parents have a powerful influence over the behavior of their children, but surprisingly some believe they just "can't do a thing."

Along with being a mom or dad comes the responsibility of training these little ones. Some children from every economic level—poor, middle-class, and rich families—are treated like weeds left to grow untended in a garden. They desperately need training physically, spiritually, emotionally, and intellectually.

Children aren't always easy to discipline. If I didn't learn that from raising my own children, I certainly learned it from counseling families. It's challenging, but incredibly essential and rewarding. What's the secret?

There are three important principles that are often overlooked in nurturing and training:

1. Motive
2. Positive expectations
3. Opportunity

These are proactive methods, not reactive, which means they require planning in advance. Here's how to use them.

Motive. It's OK to reward your child's good behavior in a tangible way. Some parents feel children should experience inner satisfaction from trying their best and doing the right thing. That's true, but there's nothing wrong with spoken rewards and gifts too. A child (and also an adult) likes praise and appropriate material rewards. Maybe your disapproval is expressed frequently through spanking, grounding, or time outs, but how often do you express your approval? A good rule is to use three comments of praise for every one of correction or punishment.

Drew and Jack, ages six and seven, couldn't remember to turn the bathroom lights off. The boys weren't trying to be disobedient, they needed a reminder that would work. I counted out twenty-five pennies for each and put them on the dining room table where they could see them often. I said they could keep the pennies after their visit, but every time they left a light on after they left a room, I'd take back a penny. Is this bribing? No. It's using a reward, a concrete symbol, to teach a household rule—and it worked!

Positive expectations. Expect the best of your children. Then stay away from negative arguments and discussions. Tell your children in advance what behavior is expected of them in a situation. "I know I'm going to be so pleased with the nice welcome you give to our relatives" or "I'll enjoy seeing your good manners at the restaurant" or "I know you can do a good job cleaning your room." Research has demonstrated that children tend to live up to the expectations parents or teachers have for them.

For your part, expect to find joy in parenthood. Contrary to feminist messages, moms, you will never regret using time and energy training your children. It's the best investment you'll ever make. Here's how it works: *training and love = awesome blessings and benefits.* Show your child(ren) that you treasure being their mom.

Opportunity. Consider the capability of your child. Make sure your requests are appropriate and that children have the ability and equipment to do what you ask. Keep your children's environment and your requirements as simple as possible. Have lots of shelves for their toys (toy boxes don't work as well for maintaining order). Alternate toys by packing a few away and bringing out a "fresh" batch. Have pegs for pajamas and clothes.

Be alert to each developmental level. I have to smile when I see a parent trying to reason with a four-year-old. The capability to think abstractly isn't developed until about age seven. Until then, children need to respond because they're capable and because you said so.

Well-trained children will be an incredible joy to you and to others. They're part of a beautiful cycle of intimate caring. When your children are young, you discover lost parts of your own childhood. When your children get older, they expand your world with their friends and activities, and when they're adults, they'll teach you things and give you interesting new perspectives. When your children have children, you have a chance to impact grandchildren's lives too. Then when you're old, the little children that you made time for, that you spent your resources on, may be the ones who care for you in your old age. That's the cycle of giving and receiving through the years.

Exploring Scripture

What has God commanded in Proverbs 22:6? "Train up a child in the way he is to go, and when he is old he will not depart from it." If you nurture your children well and guide them in right thinking, right choices, and right actions, it will stick with them.

Proverbs 12:1 says, "Whoever loves instruction loves knowledge, but he who hates correction is stupid." Teach your children that discipline is valuable and a sign of your love. And never forget, you won't be able to discipline your child(ren) well unless you discipline yourself first.

Taking Action

- Children are supposed to be a blessing and a joy! What changes in the behaviors of my children need to be made for them to begin to be blessings and joys?

- What changes do I need to make in myself to help my children change?

- How can I use positive expectations, approval, and rewards to motivate my child(ren) to make these changes?

- Record each child's name and a plan you'll try this week.

Thank You, Lord, for my precious children. Give me Your wisdom as I look at them and think about how I can train them more effectively. They are not weeds; they are tender plants growing in the garden of our home.

꧂ FORTY–EIGHT ꧁

Bonding Brothers and Sisters

$\mathcal{T}$wo boys, aged five and two, were lost in a national forest for twenty-four hours. The older brother took care of his little brother until help came. He said he was scared but didn't want to show it so his little brother wouldn't cry. What a picture of love between two so-very-young brothers! But in my counseling practice, I've also seen brothers and sisters on the verge of killing one another.

We all want to instill sibling love without rivalry in our children. But brothers and sisters, left to their own devices, can be competitive and critical of one another. Not only do they often fail to encourage one another in sports or creative work, at times they actually discourage one another with put-down remarks. Children within the same family sometimes tease one another. This teasing can become harsh and cruel when it hits the vulnerable parts of a brother or sister—it's really not done in fun at all but is a disguise for meanness. It can also be a symptom of an underlying problem of insecurity or a way to get Mom's or Dad's attention. Sometimes kids are just bored and fall into troublesome behaviors because their energies are not positively directed elsewhere.

In our home I recall a few knock-down-drag-out battles. The children competed against one another in sports and games, but overall they kept it fun. They learned love, acceptance, and compromise. Then, when our son David needed a bone marrow transplant, each of his sisters and his brother willingly underwent tests to see who could be the donor.

Tamara, a new bride of five months, was selected as the closest match. David's other sister, Pamela, a senior in college, got special permission to student teach close to home so she could care for her other brother, Dan, our junior-high-age son. I went to live near the University Hospital for two months during David's transplant. Dan visited David every weekend with games and videos for David to help make the days of isolation more pleasant.

On transplant day, all the children wanted to be present. None of the siblings complained about the disruptions to their lives during David's illness. The statue of a boy carrying his brother on his back with the inscription "He's not heavy, he's my brother" tearfully reminds me of the preciousness of sibling love.

Your children, like mine, will bond if you hold them together tightly until the bonding takes place—the same as when you glue two pieces of wood together. Yes, your children will disagree occasionally because they have different opinions. Encourage them to talk about their feelings honestly and kindly. Let them know you expect them to be different from each other but you also expect them to respect and treasure one another.

Here are some things you can do to encourage healthy bonding among your children.

1. Little children will fight; how you handle it is important. Sometimes it's best to separate them and forbid them to play together for a time, maybe an hour or two. Your children will start to long for each other and be much kinder when they play again. Or you can try sending them to the same room; they must stay there together until they can tell you how they'll solve the problem without fighting next time.

2. Take your children's pictures together often, like on the first day of school every year; take family pictures on holidays and during vacations. Stress to them that this picture shows them with their brother or sister, and they need to take care of each other. Teach family respect. Say, "You're a Rolfs (or a Smith), and it's a privilege to be part of our family."

3. Once a week, ideally on Sunday, make it family day, a time to enjoy one another. Plan activities for all the children to participate in. Enlist your husband's support. If you have more time, do the planning, but make sure your husband has an active role to play. Yes, some of your children may grumble, but just say, "Sorry, that's the plan; you have to join us." Have dinner in the dining room and make a celebration of it. Play board games in teams to make it fair (like Monopoly™ or Sherlock Holmes Baker Street™ where you try to solve a mystery). Expect everyone to enjoy one another's company. Perhaps sleep together on quilts in front of the fireplace, like a camping trip at home.

4. Insist your children value one another's ideas. Remind them that no one starts out perfect. Set firm rules that they cannot damage or destroy each other's work or possessions.

5. Plan activities where your children have to work as a team. Give them chores to share; let them divide up who should do what. Encourage them to help one another with projects.

6. Never foster sibling rivalry by favoring one child over another.

 *Exploring Scripture*

Look up Mark 1:16–19, 29. Peter and Andrew were brothers and buddies. They worked together and lived together and Jesus called the two together. Obviously these men understood Genesis 4:9 where Cain asked God, "Am I my brother's keeper?" They knew the answer was, "Yes!" As rugged outdoorsmen, Peter and Andrew would have had to look out for each other. We never read about Andrew's objecting to the Lord, "Why can't I be the rock upon which You build Your church Jesus?" No whining, "Why Peter and not me?"

James and John also were called to follow Jesus together. When their mother, the wife of Zebedee, came to Jesus to ask for good spots on either side of Jesus for her sons in the kingdom, she inquired equally for both of them. No parentally induced sibling rivalry there.

One more thing—Jesus calls us His brothers and sisters. Isn't that an awesome privilege!

Taking Action

- What have you already done successfully to bond your children and reduce sibling rivalry?

- Which of the suggestions given above might work in your home?

When a problem arises, sit down with your school-age children and discuss these problem-solving steps:

1. Review the goals: to get along with a brother and sister with love, fairness, and kindness; to avoid envy, argument, and unhealthy competition.
2. Review the circumstances that led to the problem.
3. Have them examine how they might react differently in the future to avoid the problem.
4. Think of a disagreement as a challenge to be met and resolved. Moms and dads, don't get caught in the argument.

- What do you need to do to improve the relationships with your own grown brothers and sisters?

Heavenly Father, good relationships among our children don't just "happen"; I can actively teach our children to respect each other and to work our their differences. Help me see their squabbles as opportunities for growth.

Facing the Future

When fifty-five-year-old Elsie first came to see me, she worked long hours and was too harried to do more than survive. She couldn't eliminate her job because she feared having enough money for retirement or for future medical problems.

Elsie admitted she was a driven women, scurrying around always looking ahead fearfully. Elsie had become depressed when her nest emptied. Then she further started to fear that she might lose her husband and his emotional and financial support. She feared any change and had become so paralyzed by concern over the future that she lost her delight in the present.

We all look to the future and see changes ahead—both positive and negative changes. If we have children and they leave home for good, it can be a traumatic change. And it's tough to grow older and not be able physically to do the things we once did. The future does involve losses; I encourage clients to recognize the void.

But with preparation, transitions come more smoothly. Throwing out anchors into other areas of our lives along the way helps; we need strong interests in several areas to replace the interests of our younger years. We need to continue to make new friends. And many women have developed powerful ministries in the later years of their lives when they are free from family responsibilities.

The whole retirement idea is often a trap. It can create unnatural fears and mess up our lives right now. Does God really mean for us to retire? We don't hear about Eve or Sarah retiring. Consider Caleb in his old age. Caleb pleased God because he refused to allow fear of death to govern his decisions. He put his trust in God, and God said they would enter the Promised Land. Caleb knew the danger; he had personally scouted the fortified cities and the land. He saw the giants they'd have to overcome, and he stated, "We are well able to overcome it" (Num. 13:30). How could he be so confident? Only because of his attitude of refusing to fear the future and his faith in the power of God to deal with any problem. And God rewarded Caleb.

How about Job? Did Job worry about the future even after he lost all that he had? No way! Did he ever retire? What were his latter days, the typical retirement period, like? Job 42:12, 16–17 says, "Now the LORD blessed the latter days of Job more than his beginning; for he had fourteen thousand sheep, six thousand camels, one thousand yoke of oxen, and one thousand female donkeys . . . After this Job lived one hundred and forty years, and saw his children and grandchildren for four generations. So Job died, old and full of days." Did he keep busy? Even overseeing the people who cared for all that livestock was full-time work.

Death is a reality in your future and mine, and accepting the inevitability of death is wise. Like many women, until I reached the late thirties, I seldom thought about my life having an end. Recognizing death as a fact helped me focus on living well. Death is not to be feared, nor are the unpredictable circumstances of life reason for fear. Too many women live in a nagging fear of one kind or another regarding the future while one of their biggest fears should be dying without having really lived. Women I've counseled who don't live with the full realization of death as inevitable are often far more willing to put up with unbiblical situations in their lives instead of working to change them.

We can face the future bravely by living a full, rich life every day. Every stage of life has its upside and its downside. Christ came to give peace and perspective despite anything that might happen to us in the future.

Exploring Scripture

Psalm 91:15 says, "He shall call upon Me, and I will answer him; I will be with him in trouble, I will deliver him and honor him."

- What does God promise to do if trouble comes?

Some excellent verses for meditation as we face the future without fear are:

- First Corinthians 2:9: "But as it is written [in Isaiah 64:4]: 'Eye has not seen, nor ear heard, nor have entered into the heart of man the things which God has prepared for those who love Him.'"
- Psalm 16:11: "You will show me the path of life; in Your presence is fullness of joy; at Your right hand are pleasures forevermore."

Taking Action

- Now be honest. What concerns you about the future?

- Complete this prayer: "Dear Lord, help me to trust You concerning. . . ."

- What areas of your life do you still need to give to God?

Lord, the future appears to hold less family responsibilities and more free time, yet often one's later years are filled with illness and financial concerns. Thank You that I can rest in You both now and in the future—that the path I am on will never be without Your love and presence.

৯ঽ FIFTY ৶৽

Worshiping God

*W*orship is the intimate expression of ardent love. Scripture says that God promises to inhabit, to live in, the worship and praises of His people.

Why do we worship? Out of awe for God's creation? Recently, due to the study of genetics and DNA, scientists have had to acknowledge the facts of Genesis that all mankind came from one man and one woman and that the first human was made of clay just as Genesis described. God desires our worship because He is our Creator.

So God made us and the beautiful world around us. But that's not all. He sent His Son to atone when we messed up. (If you're a mom, think about it—which of your children would you sacrifice if their life could save the whole world?) And then amazingly Jesus was willing to die for the world. Did Jesus really die and rise from the dead like that? There were witnesses, thousands who watched His crucifixion and saw Him after He arose. If we don't believe that, we may as well deny the whole record of history. There's more evidence for the life, death, and resurrection of Christ than for much of what children learn from history books today.

So worship is in order, but how? In public or private, at church or at home, at work, all throughout our days, are we aware that the living God is with us? We do a fair amount of talking each day both aloud and in our heads. How much of it is *to* God? How would we like it if somebody came to see us and they talked about us as if we weren't present at all? Eerie? That's the impression I get in some churches I visit. Beautiful songs are sung about God but not *to* Him.

How do you worship God? Have you ever tried raising your hands as you pray? Are you concerned about looking dumb? God won't think so. At first it may feel awkward, but soon it's a natural expression of lifting your mind and heart to God. Try it at home or sit in the back row of church on Sunday if you're worried others will watch. (They may decide to try it, too.)

Moses held his hands up to bring victory in battle; Jesus stretched His hand forth to heal; lifting is symbolic of dedicating your hands and your entire self to God.

In Isaiah 6:1–4 the prophet Isaiah saw the Lord high and raised up. Because of that vision he was changed permanently. God became the focus of his life. I wonder how many times Isaiah, in his private worship, relived those moments in his mind? Is that vision what gave him confidence to go on when the people rejected him and misunderstood his message? What if you started your worship with the memory of a time when you were aware of God's unmistakable, undeniable real presence in your life? I often use the picture of myself in a hospital chapel surrendering my sick son to God but imploring Him to save his life.

Another time I was prayed for in an atmosphere where I felt the presence of God ever so strongly. The person prayed, "Let there be more of God and less of 'you,'" which I took to mean less of my pride, selfishness, and defensiveness which had been my private desire for some time. After the prayer I lay on the floor flat on my back worshiping God and repeating over and over in awe, "In His presence is the fullness of joy." I've never felt so close to His glory. I wanted to stay there forever, but twenty minutes was all I had. I'll remember them all my life.

You may have had more or less dramatic experiences of God's presence. But think back to when you've known God was there. Afterwards maybe you said you must have imagined it, but then you knew. Treasure those moments, dwell on them when you start to pray.

Reesa found it difficult to worship God and enter into His presence because of memories from her past that popped into her head when her mind was still. A little voice whispered, "Not you, you're not worthy, remember such and such?"

She fought these thoughts, but the harder she tried, the stronger the thoughts became. I explained, "Reesa, you want to simply discard the past like a bag of old clothes, but God wants you to cut the past up and keep what's usable in your wardrobe of the future." We all have experiences we'd like to forget forever, but God in His wisdom reweaves them and makes a prettier fabric than before. I've learned to appreciate His designs.

When you close your eyes to pray in church, close your mind as well to the things of the world. Let your worship be real, not a mere ritual. When you get to heaven, will it matter if you raised your hands or knelt or lay flat to worship? No, it will be important that you loved God and that you loved others. However best you can worship God, do it. Where does God dwell today? In the praises of His people! Worship God because He alone is worthy to be praised.

We were created to be in fellowship with God, not do work for God. We might as well learn to enjoy worship here, because that's what we'll be doing forever in heaven.

 Exploring Scripture

In Matthew 2 the Magi demonstrate the proper method of worship:

- Nothing stood in the way of the Magi's reaching Jesus.
- They thoughtfully planned their gifts in advance.
- When they found Jesus, they were filled with joy.
- They bowed and worshiped Him humbly.
- After worshiping, they presented their gifts.

Look up Colossians 2:16: "Therefore do not let anyone judge you by what you eat or drink, or with regard to a religious festival, a New Moon celebration or a Sabbath day" (NIV).

- Is it right to judge the worship style of others? The traditions of other Christians may be different; it's not *how* you worship but that you truly *do worship* that matters.

Taking Action

Give your children opportunities to join you in your acts of worship. Plan a special family worship service at home.

Experiment with other forms of worship. Write a song or praise letter to God. Worship Him as you load the dishwasher—praise the Lord for the equipment, the soap that you don't have to make yourself, the healthy bodies that ate this food on these dirty dishes. Read how Brother Lawrence in the classic book *The Practice of the Presence of God* worshiped God in all his daily chores.

❦

Lord, may I never forget that I was created for fellowship with You and not created to do work for You. I need to practice here on earth what I will be doing in heaven—praising You.

❧ FIFTY–ONE ❧

Being a Grandma

*W*hy is Scripture so big on lineage? Over and over there are lists of ancestors. It's because of the incredible impact we all have on future generations. I used to think doting grandparents were strange. Didn't they have enough going on in their own lives? Now that I'm older, I see the value of being an actively involved grandparent. What kind of grandchildren do you want? You can be involved in their development.

God expects us to set a good example for grandchildren to follow. I want my grandchildren to remember me as someone who loved the Lord and them wildly. Children are unconditionally loved by God, but they often first experience His love through their parents and their grandparents.

Sometimes a parent or a grandparent dies before little children grow up. I wonder if there is an intercessory prayer function for believers in heaven. I don't know about heaven, but I do know I have intercessory work here. Every morning my husband and I pray for our grown children's and grandchildren's safety and protection throughout the day. We pray they will learn only that which is emotionally, physically, and spiritually sound. We also pray that they'll forget anything that isn't wholesome and worth remembering.

I love seeing my grandchildren regularly, preferably when their parents leave them with us for a few days so we can enjoy them fully. (It's hard to give attention to your children and grandchildren at the same time.) We grandparents have a powerful role as encouragers and back-up trainers, but we must not be quick to intrude and assume parenting responsibilities that are not ours. The primary trainers are parents.

Here are some tips for being a wonderful grandma.

- Let your grandchildren know you have expectations for their behavior.

    Don't be just a "yes" person to a child. Be willing to discipline when you must. Overindulgence is not fair to their parents, plus it undermines consistency if there's a contrast between your discipline style and what your grandchildren experience at home.

- In order to be an encourager you need to focus on each child individually.

  You have time to study each child's personality differences, talents, interests, and skills. This will help you select books and activities geared to outside interests. Adapt activities to a child's abilities so that you can help foster each child's uniqueness.

- Praise your grandchildren's parents for any good you observe in your grandchildren—polite manners, a kind gesture, a good habit that you see.

  Your adult children need to hear about signs of successful parenting; it's easy for parents to become discouraged. Who's in a better position to tell them their parenting is working than you? Incidentally, if you haven't told your children about God in their youth or they weren't open to hearing, present the Gospel to them now as adults. They may be more receptive to hearing once they are searching for truth to teach their children.

- Tactfully make parenting suggestions you feel are appropriate.

  If you think the parents are being too strict or too lenient with one of the grandchildren, say, "Maybe I'm wrong—I know I only observe a small bit of your behavior and interactions—but do you think possibly . . .?" Be as nonjudgmental and noncritical as you possibly can. It's true; you don't see everything, but do share your thoughts. And model in front of your adult children healthy parental interactions with the grandchildren.

- Keep alert to your grandchildren's stages.

  Refresh your memory with books on child development. You've been through it, but you forget, and some things you and I didn't learn.

- Keep a bin of art materials and age-appropriate toys in your home.

  Make a special place for books. Be sure the grandchildren always clean up before they go home. Remember, you're trying to instill good habits.

- Have special date or appointment times.

  If you live close to your grandchildren, each week take one child alone for a special time together. Play a game after dinner or plan an outing your grandchild will enjoy. This helps grandpa have time, too, instead of only grandma developing relationships with the grandchildren.

- Do whatever it takes to keep in communication no matter how greatly you're separated by distance.

  Use letters, postcards, tapes, videos, or e-mail with computer-literate grandchildren. With our postal system and technology, it's never been easier to keep a long-distance relationship strong.

Grandchildren often become such a vital part of our lives that we can't imagine the world without them. "Well done, good and faithful servants" includes grandparenting tasks as well. If children are arrows in the quiver, what are grandchildren—the arrowheads that will penetrate the future?

 Exploring Scripture

Read 2 Timothy 1:5: "When I call to remembrance the genuine faith that is in you, which dwelt first in your grandmother Lois and your mother Eunice, and I am persuaded is in you also." Timothy's faith was a result of prayer and Christian training of his mother and grandmother. Wouldn't you like this to be said about you and your grandchildren?

Taking Action

Your number one action will always be praying for your grandchildren. Write their names on a daily prayer list and keep it by your bed (I paste their pictures on it, too). Pray for each of them by name before your feet hit the floor in the morning.

- Which of the suggestions above might work for your family?

- If you're a mother, what can you do to involve your children's grandparents more directly in their grandchildren's lives?

❧

Thank You, Lord, for my precious grandchildren. Thank You for their parents, my dearly loved children. May my prayers and actions on their behalf always lead us all closer to You.

Experiencing Contentment

Feelings and circumstances change. I wish each of you readers could spend some time sitting in my counseling chair. You'd hear a woman with a handsome husband say she doesn't find him physically attractive, women with attentive husbands complaining their husbands always want to know everything they're doing, women with workaholic husbands who complain their husbands don't make enough money. Some women desire to marry, but the right man doesn't come along. Others marry and wish they hadn't.

The point is that during some periods of life, your husband may seem like the most wonderful man in the world; at other times you're sure he's a schmo. Your children may be your greatest joy or your toughest trial. Your husband is never home as much as you'd like. Then one day he retires and all of a sudden he's around too much. Nothing stays the same, least of all your feelings. Circumstances will never be humanly perfect here.

But Jesus Christ is the same yesterday, today, and tomorrow. No matter what is happening in our lives, we can experience ten thousand joys in Him if we look to Him for our contentment, our approval, our pleasure.

Some women live with very difficult circumstances. When Cleo was a young woman in her thirties, she used to daydream that her drunken, abusive husband would die. He badmouthed her to others even at church, and everyone thought she was the "bad guy" in their marriage who caused him to drink. Christ comforted her and motivated her to pray for her husband. Cleo did the Christlike thing. She didn't feel love for her husband, but she knew God did. Christ gave her the peace and contentment she needed to enjoy life despite her circumstances.

Cleo learned to listen to God and live in the minute. She kept focused on Jesus for her esteem instead of trying to justify her actions to others. After thirty-five years of marriage, Cleo's husband joined AA. He became a Christian in reality, not just in word, and started behaving like a tender husband. When he died several years later, Cleo couldn't imagine life without him. Once again her relationship with God kept her from being disconsolate and gave her the ability to continue living joyfully.

In contrast, Dana talked constantly about leaving her insensitive and critical husband. Dana was a Christian and wouldn't divorce him, but her homelife was miserable. For years she complained to anyone who would listen. Dana said, "I no longer feel any love for my husband."

I told Dana, "Treat him as if you love him because you made a vow before God to love him as long as you both shall live, and vows made before God are not to be broken. As you act that way, your feelings may change. Even if they don't, you're honoring God by your obedience and He will bless you." I didn't suggest that she hide her feelings, only that she control them.

Dana continued to moan about her unsatisfied emotional goals, household tasks her husband didn't complete, and family needs neglected. Dana's childhood memories of her parents' quarreling made her feel guilty about her griping, but nevertheless she repeated for her children the patterns of family life she'd hated. Needless to say, Dana never experienced contentment in her life. She refused to move past her anger and bitterness.

Each woman has a choice to make—contentment in Christ or dissatisfaction with life. Feelings and behaviors can be brought under control and changed by an act of the will. There's a popular saying that feelings are neither right nor wrong, they simply are. *What we do with those feelings can be very right or very wrong.*

Because feelings change, it's important to base our lives on truth, not feelings. We can't let our happiness rest on the behavior or words of others. We must base our primary happiness and joy on our relationship with Jesus Christ.

However, I do need to warn about abuse once again. Basing your joy and happiness on Jesus Christ alone doesn't mean you are to allow yourself to be physically abused. You need to seek professional help to learn how to stop the abuse and preserve your marriage. A professional will evaluate the causes of the abusive behavior. (See 30, "Surviving Your Husband's Life Crises.")

Contrary to popular psychology, most men and women should be able to handle verbal abuse without being devastated. Remember the old saying, "Sticks and stones will break my bones, but words will never hurt me"? The Lord can help you hear verbal abuse and maintain healthy self-esteem. Very often a husband's verbal abuse stems from his own lack of inner security. Certainly this is undesirable, and a wife must pray for her husband's emotional growth. Typically her pleas alone will not motivate him to behave differently, and he needs outside help. These are extreme, but far too frequent, problems.

No matter what your situation, it's never impossible or too late to begin to experience contentment. Perhaps you've never been married.

Or you've lost your husband through divorce or death, and you're grieving for the past. Soak in the security of the constant things in your life now. The sun rises every day for you. Night creeps over each day to refresh you. Sleep gives the new start of each new tomorrow. And Christ is present to husband you perfectly whatever your condition.

Remember contentment is not the same as complacency. You always need to change what's within your ability to change and develop yourself into the best you can be.

Exploring Scripture

What does Ecclesiastes 3:1–8 say about experiencing contentment in the present? It says there's a time to have babies and a time to be done, a time for saving and a time for garage sales and moving, a time to be sad and a time to be glad, a time to be patient and a time to speak, a time to build houses and a time to sell, and a time for . . . whatever is going on in your life right now.

Ask God for the wisdom He promises in James 1:5 for your present situations. Accept what you must, and embrace all that life holds for you because it's been allowed by God. Knowing God is in charge, you can go through the cycles of your life with confidence and contentment.

Taking Action

- Describe an example from your own marriage when you've needed to change your feelings so that you could experience contentment in your relationship.

- How can you find greater contentment with God?

- With yourself?

- With your husband?

- With your family?

- With friends and acquaintances?

Lord, I have a choice to be discontent with everything around me or to find my contentment in You. It's a choice I make with my will. May I be content, not passive or complacent. May I control my feelings, not hide or suppress them. My peace and joy come from You. May I daily choose to keep my promises.

Epilogue

ifty-two ways to help us keep our promises and our commitments on the run of life! I'm wondering how you feel now—overwhelmed? Or motivated and encouraged, as I hope. We're all running together, and I'd love for you to drop me a note and let me know how you're doing. Remember it takes a whole life to learn how to run the Christian race well. God has given you signposts along the way to keep you going in the right direction and making the right choices. He also wants you to run at your own speed, at your own natural pace, and to have fun, to experience joy, along the way.

Now that I've come to the end of this book, I've asked God if there's anything I need to add. I feel He's said, "Tell the women I love them, say it again, I love them. I delight in them as they are, and I'll help them become what they can be. Remind them these ways aren't a 'To Do' list. They're not supposed to be hard; they're supposed to be fun. And remind the women to laugh a lot. Laughter is the music of heaven, and these women are My joy."